"My sons can tell you about the Saturday mornings when I used to take them out for breakfast and for what I called 'manhood training.' I realized it was my job to help them grow from boyhood to the responsibilities of mature manhood. How I wish I'd had Marty's book back then. I'm so glad today's dads have this invaluable tool to use with their sons."

Bob Lepine, Cohost, FamilyLife Today

"*Brave and Bold: 31 Devotions to Strengthen Men* is a basic training manual for biblical manhood. Machowski offers thirty-one essential characteristics of biblical manhood in this compact, accessible devotional. Men who read this work and take on the challenges contained in it will be blessed and grow far beyond the thirty-one days it is designed to cover."

Curtis Solomon, Executive Director of the Biblical Counseling Coalition; Cofounder of Solomon Soul Care

"As the father of five now-grown sons, I was called to the man-raising business. Had this book been around when my sons were younger, it would have been part of our manhood curriculum. It expresses what men are meant to be—and what I still want to be when I grow up. *Brave and Bold* is solid, practical, biblical, and accessible. Marty combines great illustrations with biblical insight, and then adds recommended next steps for application. Get it. Read it. Do it."

Tim Shorey, Author of *Respect the Image: Reflecting Human Worth in How We Listen and Talk, 30/30 Hindsight: 30 Reflections on a 30-Year Headache*, and *An ABC Prayer to Jesus: Praise for Hearts Both Young and Old*

"I thank God for *Brave and Bold*. It provides an antidote to one of the primary spiritual problems for men of our day: complacency. The church is not a passive organization to be tossed about by the whims of a pagan world. Rather, the church is a militant army, marching against the enemy on a mission for God. Marty reminds us of that in a loving, pastoral way, challenging men to be soldiers for Christ!"

Major O.J. DiIulio, Retired Army chaplain

"Marty Machowski has written a thoroughly biblical, highly practical, and enjoyable book that will encourage men, young and old, to pursue godly manhood. I know Marty personally and he is the kind of man I would be honored for my sons to grow up to be like. I highly recommend this book to anyone who wants to rise above the misguided versions of manhood presented in society and wishes to capture a biblical vision for manhood. Pick up a copy today—you will be blessed!"

Josh Mulvihill, President of Gospel Shaped Family; author of *Biblical Grandparenting* and *Preparing Children for Marriage*

"As a father of four boys, I am exceedingly thankful for *Brave and Bold*. Machowski has produced a timely, winsome, understandable, grace-infused, biblically saturated devotional for men of all ages. As Christian men desperately need compassionate and compelling guidance, *Brave and Bold* offers a clear path toward God-honoring biblical manhood. Whether used for personal devotion, group study, or parenting, Machowski's work will undoubtedly bless and challenge you!"

J. Aaron White, Pastor for Teaching and Training, Redeemer Bible Church, Minnetonka, MN; author of *Man Up, Kneel Down: Shepherding Your Wife Toward Greater Joy in Jesus* and *Paul's Big Letter: A Kid-Friendly Journey Through Romans*

"We all know Marty is one of today's preeminent authors for gospel-centered children's and family literature. Now he has blessed the church with a fantastic resource for men. *Brave and Bold* is refreshing spiritual boot camp for both young believers and longtime Christians—never heavy-handed, never watered down, always grace-filled, and brimming with applicable truth. Pick up a copy! I have already recommended it to several churches I know."

Joshua Cooley, *New York Times* bestselling author of *Creator, Father, King: A One Year Journey With God*, *Heroes of the Bible Devotional*, and *The Biggest Win*

BRAVE AND BOLD

31 Devotions to Strengthen Men

Marty Machowski

New
Growth
Press

newgrowthpress.com

New Growth Press, Greensboro, NC 27404
newgrowthpress.com
Copyright © 2021 by Marty Machowski

Unless otherwise noted, Scripture quotations are taken from *The Holy Bible, English Standard Version*®. Copyright © 2000; 2001 by Crossway Bibles, a division of Good News Publishers. Used by permission. All rights reserved.

Scripture quotations marked NIV are taken from THE HOLY BIBLE, NEW INTERNATIONAL VERSION®, NIV® Copyright © 1973, 1978, 1984, 2011 by Biblica, Inc.® Used by permission. All rights reserved worldwide.

Scripture quotations marked NKJV are taken from the New King James Version®. Copyright © 1982 by Thomas Nelson. Used by permission. All rights reserved.

Scripture quotations marked NLT are taken from the Holy Bible, New Living Translation, copyright © 1996, 2004, 2015 by Tyndale House Foundation. Used by permission of Tyndale House Publishers, Inc., Carol Stream, Illinois 60188. All rights reserved.

Scripture quotations marked NASB are taken from the New American Standard Bible®, Copyright © 1960, 1971, 1977, 1995, 2020 by The Lockman Foundation. All rights reserved.

Cover Design: Faceout Books, faceoutstudio.com
Interior Design and Typesetting: Gretchen Logterman

ISBN: 978-1-64507-069-6 (Print)
ISBN: 978-1-64507-098-6 (eBook)

Library of Congress Cataloging-in-Publication Data

Names: Machowski, Martin, 1963- author.
Title: Brave and bold : 31 devotions to strengthen men / Marty Machowski.
Description: Greensboro, NC : New Growth Press, [2021] | Includes
  bibliographical references. | Summary: "In Brave and Bold, Marty
  Machowski offers thirty-one daily readings to encourage you to become a
  man whose strength comes from following Jesus and reflects him to a
  watching world"-- Provided by publisher.
Identifiers: LCCN 2020051048 (print) | LCCN 2020051049 (ebook) | ISBN
  9781645070696 (print) | ISBN 9781645070986 (ebook)
Subjects: LCSH: Men--Religious life--Meditations.
Classification: LCC BV4528.2 .M28 2021 (print) | LCC BV4528.2 (ebook) |
  DDC 242/.642--dc23
LC record available at https://lccn.loc.gov/2020051048
LC ebook record available at https://lccn.loc.gov/2020051049

Printed in the United States of America

28 27 26 25 24 23 22 21   1 2 3 4 5

Dedication

I would like to dedicate this book to the memory of
my father, Thaddeus Joseph Machowski, who passed
on into glory October 16th, 2020. No other man
influenced my life more than him.

My father ran the race of faith with grace and finished
well; he remained faithful to his family and his God.
In his last days, he shared his faith with the aid
assisting in his care. In our last conversation, he told
me, "People ask me if I am afraid to die. I say, 'Afraid
to die? Why should I be afraid to die? I'm going home
to be with Jesus!'"

Dad, thank you for your consistent example of
love, generosity, and grace toward God and others.
I learned to be faithful by watching you model
faithfulness as a husband and father over the years.
And there is no doubt that I've been sustained by
your prayers. You've left big shoes to fill, but by God's
grace, I will follow Christ, the way you did, with grace
and strength, until my final breath.

Contents

Introduction

I remember the day Uncle Joe took my brother and me, along with our cousin Danny, fishing. One of us knocked over the water jug. We argued over who should pick it up while the day's water supply poured out like an open fire hose. Uncle Joe ran over and righted the jug. Then he pointed to his size 14 clodhoppers and said, "You see this boot? If you don't stop fooling around, you will find this boot in your backside!" While it was clear to us that Uncle Joe never intended to carry out his threat, his warnings curbed our foolishness and helped us boys to take responsibility and become men. Those outings were more than recreation; my uncle wanted to see his nephews, along with his son, grow to be men—honorable, responsible men. The time he sacrificed to spend with us and take us on regular outings inspired me to spend time doing similar things with my own sons.

Manhood is not about strength or stature; biblical manhood is about character—leading, serving, being responsible, protecting, and providing. More than any other area, we are called to lead in our love and worship of God. Think of King David, too small of stature to be presented to Samuel for consideration for king. His gifts? He wrote poetry and played music. But God describes him as "a man after his [my] own heart" (1 Samuel 13:14). David may have been small of stature, but his trust in the Lord led to his defeat of Goliath with nothing more than a sling and a stone.

Men are not born; boys are. Manhood requires education, development, and application. You can learn the skills of manhood by reading and applying the Scriptures and by watching and listening to other men as they lead. Or you can ignore that instruction and learn by life's consequences in the school of hard knocks.

Joining the Army accelerated my manhood education. Every basic training recruit there benefited from a good old-fashioned kick in the pants now and again. At least that was my drill sergeant's philosophy. Except the way he said it was not quite so diplomatic. From the moment I was assigned to Bravo Company till the day I left for home, Sergeant Harris spent his days getting us ready for war. While I never saw combat, the lessons Sergeant Harris taught me helped me to become a man.

The Army transformed me from a scrawny, couldn't-do-more-than-ten-push-ups, put-off-until-tomorrow procrastinator into a leader. Harris didn't accept excuses. He pushed our platoon beyond our comfort zone. A weight lifter doesn't get stronger by lifting less. He adds ten pounds to the bar and strains every sinew to press it. Harris added the ten pounds and then shouted it up with his encouragement to not quit. In the end, he helped us all raise the bar.

Many days we thought he pushed us farther than we could run. But each time we arrived at our destination, we realized our expectations were too low. Harris wasn't just mean (although we sure wondered); every law, including detailed directions for rolling up our T-shirts and underwear, had a purpose. It wasn't an attempt to glorify order or make his platoon look good; his rules provided the discipline we needed for survival in war. Though I never fired my M-16 at a person, I would learn that all of life is a battle. I would appreciate the discipline that came with a veiled affection from the man with the trooper hat.

Introduction

Harris loved his job, and he loved his recruits. He knew how to change the inflection in his voice so that you knew he loved you while he was yelling. As the weeks passed, I came to discern the encouragement hidden behind his harsh charges. On graduation day, no one stood prouder of our little grid of soldiers, all lined up on the parade field and standing at attention, than Sergeant Harris. I don't know whether Harris was a Christian, but if so, I'm sure his favorite Bible verse would have been 1 Corinthians 16:13: "Be watchful, stand firm in the faith, act like men, be strong."

The truth is that mature manhood requires every one of us to stay on top of our game. While some countries, like Israel, still have mandatory military service for everyone over eighteen years of age, there are a ton of guys who grow up without a dad or Uncle Joe or Sergeant Harris to model manhood and insist they follow. Guys who grow from boy to man without mentorship face the temptation to coast, take it easy, and go slack. Today too many of our young men fritter away valuable time fighting computer gaming battles online. More than a hundred billion dollars are spent annually by gamers across the world.[1] Hours and even days are sacrificed to artificial wars where gamers always live to play another day, even if their characters die.

While you may not be a military kind of a guy, I hope my illustrations and stories of warriors, army life, and battle will serve you nonetheless. Think of *Brave and Bold* as one older guy passing on what he has learned through the years. I pray this book can help you grow in manhood and align your priorities with what is truly most important. Think of it as manhood basic training. While each topic only takes a few minutes to read, you'll discover that the entries in these pages can take a lifetime to apply.

There are a few ways to use this book. You can read it straight through and choose two or three areas to apply. Or you can move through at a slower pace. Start at the beginning with

Brave and Bold

challenge #1 and take the following week to put it into practice. Do that every week for thirty-one weeks. Then, after you complete the last challenge, keep the book on hand to use as a refresher. On any given day, pick up the book and read the entry number that matches the calendar day of the month. Be sure to read and consider the action steps found at the end of each entry. The Get Started action step provides a Scripture to meditate on, along with a simple application that anyone can fit into his schedule. The Take the Challenge section provides you with a more challenging test and application.

Each of the daily exhortations begins with a Scripture and then moves to a story or illustration. Many of these are taken from my experiences in the Army or other military themes. (I've changed some names of people in my personal stories to protect their identities.) Each entry also contains a brief Scripture study on the topic at hand and ends with a challenge to apply the study. As James says, "be doers of the word, and not hearers only, deceiving yourselves" (1:22). Consider this book your pocket biblical manhood boot camp.

Turn the page if you're ready to enlist in this study. But once you do, I don't want you quitting on me after a few days; purpose now to finish this book. Reading is the key to unlocking the truth that God revealed to us through his Son Jesus. It is through our study of the Word that we come to love God and the gospel that has the power to transform our lives. Every man is called by God to worship, and our study of God's Word teaches us who he is and why we should worship him. The call upon every man is to move from knowing about God to loving him. Worship is the core principle that governs the heart of every man—and this is where we begin our study.

4

1

Men Worship God

"Therefore let us be grateful for receiving a kingdom that
cannot be shaken, and thus let us offer to God acceptable
worship, with reverence and awe, for our God is a
consuming fire." (Hebrews 12:28–29)

President Lincoln found himself drawing near to God amid
the Gettysburg conflict.[1] "In the stress and pinch of the
campaign there, I went to my room, and got down on my knees
and prayed God Almighty for victory at Gettysburg. I told him
that this was his country, and the war was his war, but that we
really couldn't stand another Fredericksburg or Chancellorsville.
And then and there I made a solemn vow with my Maker that
if He would stand by you boys at Gettysburg I would stand by
him. And he did, and I will!"[2]

The true measure of a man's affection can be observed in
his day-to-day pursuits and the things that capture his attention
the fullest. Do his affections for God run to the core of who he
is, or has something else captivated his attention and devotion?
Where does he invest his energy, money, and time? Watch what
excites him, what makes him angry, what makes him cry, and
you will discover the object of his worship.

What do you worship? Who or what has your highest measure of devotion? *Worship* is a word that aptly describes any of
our loves. The key is discovering what we love most. If we love
God most and all else falls in line, then we do indeed worship
God. But when anything receives our highest praise over God,

it becomes an idol. The great pastor and writer Aiden Tozer said, "What comes into our minds when we think about God is the most important thing about us. . . Worship is pure or base as the worshiper entertains high or low thoughts of God."[3]

Whatever you love or want most will control what you do and determine what you live for. If we live for our kid's performance in sports, our lives will revolve around athletics. If we live for success, we'll give ourselves to our job and work more than anyone else in our company to prove our dedication. We can give our greatest affections to impressing a beautiful woman, building a ripped physique, or even to conquering a video game, instead of to God. Anything can become the center of our life and displace God—what the Bible calls an idol.

Our love for God and our love for idols are connected; when one increases, the other decreases. Jesus said you can't serve two masters. You will love one and hate the other (Luke 16:13).

When a rich man inquired of Jesus about what he needed to do to inherit eternal life, Jesus told him to obey the commandments. The man replied that he had kept the commandments. Jesus didn't disagree with him. The problem was that the man didn't obey out of love for God but more out of obligation. Jesus's final words to the rich young ruler were some of the most challenging words ever spoken: "Go, sell everything you have and give to the poor, and you will have treasure in heaven. Then come, follow me" (Mark 10:21 NIV). Jesus knew he worshipped his money more than he did God.

What is Jesus trying to get at? Very simply, a man must love God more and worship him more—more than money, more than possessions, more than a job, more than his wife, his kids, or his free time. Whatever you love, you must love God more. If not, you'll be drawn away from God to serve worldly things. No one can serve two masters (Matthew 6:24). Jesus said he will love one and hate the other. And our love dictates what we live for. That is why we must strive to love God more than people or things. We should purpose to love him more today than we did yesterday and long to draw nearer his throne tomorrow.

Get Started

Take time today to meditate on Romans 14:11–12: "For it is written, 'As I live, says the Lord, every knee shall bow to me, and every tongue shall confess to God.' So then each of us will give an account of himself to God."

You'll never be a true man unless you come to grips with what it means to be a human made in God's image. We have all rebelled and sinned against God. But in the man Christ Jesus, we find not only forgiveness but also a covering in Christ's righteousness. If you haven't yet placed your trust in Christ, call out in a simple prayer to him, and he will reveal himself to you through the Scriptures in this study. It is only as redeemed sinners empowered by God's Spirit that we can learn what it means to be truly human.

Ask the Spirit of God to help you see what is competing for first place in your affections. What most stands in the way of you loving God more? We all have things that threaten to take our hearts captive. What do you live for? Do you live for your work? Do you live for your own comfort? If you examine your heart and ask God to show you your idols, he will. Once you discover what they are, refuse to live for them. Put God first.

Take the Challenge

After you uncover the area of your life that you are tempted to love more than God, you've got to do more than just make a change for a day. To keep God as your top priority, daily repent of your misguided affection. Consider whether Jesus is calling you, like the rich young ruler, to readjust your priorities. That could mean giving up a whole season of sports or a promotion at work, canceling a membership, limiting your involvement in an activity, or cutting out just about anything from alcohol to ice cream. In short, get radical and love God more.

2

Men Trust God

"Some trust in chariots and some in horses, but we trust in the name of the Lord our God." (Psalm 20:7)

Imagine you and a band of loyal soldiers are in the wilderness, on the run from a fierce enemy. You take refuge in a cave and plan to rest in the dark inner passages. Then you hear someone say, "I'll be out in a bit. I'm going to relieve myself in this cave." You recognize the voice immediately. It is the commander of the enemy army, alone and unaware. Kill him and you secure instant victory. You sneak up with a knife in your hand, and he would have no idea you are there in the pitch black. What would you do?

That is the true story of David (of Goliath fame) standing over King Saul in the cave of Adullam. You can read the fascinating story in 1 Samuel 24. One swipe of the knife and David could have defeated Saul. But instead of killing Saul, David cut off a piece of his robe to prove he was innocent, still loyal to God's anointed king. David trusted the Lord to win his victory and would not take matters into his own hands. David followed Saul out of the cave, declared his innocence, and offered the cloth as proof saying, "Behold, this day your eyes have seen how the Lord gave you today into my hand in the cave. And some told me to kill you, but I spared you. I said, 'I will not put out my hand against my lord, for he is the Lord's anointed'" (1 Samuel 24:10). It was then that Saul knew he had been defeated. Saul wept, confessed his wickedness, and said, "I know that you shall surely be king, and that the kingdom of Israel shall be established in your hand" (1 Samuel 24:20).

David's example in the cave and the psalms he wrote springing from his life experiences teach us the importance of trusting God in all of life. We say we trust God, but what do we do when life's trials bear down on us. Is prayer our first resort? When the challenges of life press in on all sides, can we rest knowing God is in control and he can deliver us?

David turned his prayer in that cave into a song. David prayed, "Attend to my cry, for I am brought very low! Deliver me from my persecutors, for they are too strong for me! Bring me out of prison, that I may give thanks to your name!" (Psalm 142:6–7). When life's challenges press into you like an enemy, do you trust God to deliver you, or do you look to try to press in by your own strength? Do you work harder, argue more forcefully, or resort to dishonesty, bitterness, or just plain giving up?

Godly men know they don't control their future. God is in control. They don't decide the outcome of a battle; God does. Peter tells us to follow the example of Christ, who, "When he was reviled, he did not revile in return; when he suffered, he did not threaten, but continued entrusting himself to him who judges justly" (1 Peter 2:23).

Our courage comes from entrusting our lives to God and following his ways. Solomon said, "Trust in the LORD with all your heart, and do not lean on your own understanding. In all your ways acknowledge him, and he will make straight your paths" (Proverbs 3:5–6). Are you fearful of an unknown future outcome? Trust the Lord. Are you suffering in the midst of trial, or are you mistreated? Entrust yourself to the one who judges justly.

Get Started

Take time today to meditate on Proverbs 3:5–6: "Trust in the LORD with all your heart, and do not lean on your own understanding. In all your ways acknowledge him, and he will make straight your paths."

Commit this verse to memory and make it the subject of your prayers. Bring your fears, anxieties, uncertainties, and confusion about your life or circumstances to the Lord, and entrust yourself to your God who judges justly. While God does not guarantee a trial-free life, we can be sure he will use every trial for our good and his glory in our lives.

Take the Challenge

Ask a friend to join you on a study of David's life. Read through 1 Samuel, 2 Samuel, and the book of Psalms (most of which David wrote). Keep a journal and record everything you learn from David's life—both his successes and failures—about trusting God.

3

Men Pray

"The effective, fervent prayer of a righteous man
avails much." (James 5:16 NKJV)

Desmond Doss, a combat medic who refused to carry a weapon
into battle, was the only conscientious objector to receive the
Medal of Honor for bravery during WWII. The opening paragraph of his citation describes his actions:

> He was a company aid man when the 1st Battalion
> assaulted a jagged escarpment, 400 feet high. As our
> troops gained the summit, a heavy concentration of
> artillery, mortar and machine-gun fire crashed into
> them, inflicting approximately 75 casualties and
> driving the others back. Private First Class Doss refused to seek cover and remained in the fire-swept
> area with the many stricken, carrying them 1 by 1 to
> the edge of the escarpment and there lowering them
> on a rope-supported litter down the face of a cliff to
> friendly hands. On 2 May, he exposed himself to
> heavy rifle and mortar fire in rescuing a wounded man
> 200 yards forward of the lines on the same escarpment; and 2 days later he treated 4 men who had been
> cut down while assaulting a strongly defended cave,
> advancing through a shower of grenades to within
> 8 yards of enemy forces in a cave's mouth, where he

dressed his comrades' wounds before making 4 separate trips under fire to evacuate them to safety.[1]

When asked how he was able to rescue so many men, Desmond pointed to the power of prayer. "I was praying the whole time. I just kept praying, Lord, please help me get one more. When I got this, I prayed, please help me get one more."[2] Desmond's trust and faith in Christ, demonstrated through prayer, gave him the courage to stand amid horrific adversity. The men who railed at him for refusing to carry a rifle couldn't deny the power of prayer that saved many of their lives. Desmond's prayers revealed profound courage. He didn't pray for the bullets to miss him; he prayed to save one more. If God granted that request, the bullets became irrelevant. Desmond understood that prayer connected him to the all-powerful Creator of the universe.

Prayer is simply the daily conversation we have with God. Jesus introduced a revolutionary concept when he taught the disciples to pray. God, he explained, is our loving Father, eager to answer our prayers. Jesus said, "But when you pray, go into your room, close the door and pray to your Father, who is unseen. Then your Father, who sees what is done in secret, will reward you. And when you pray, do not keep on babbling like pagans, for they think they will be heard because of their many words. Do not be like them, for your Father knows what you need before you ask him" (Matthew 6:6–8 NIV). Then Jesus went on to teach the disciples the Lord's prayer (6:9–13).

Since God the Father knows what we need even before we ask, why do we have to pray? Why doesn't God just give us what we need? For starters, there is a big difference between what we *need* and what we *want*. Men want the treasures of the world, but what they need is God himself. If God is the most excellent treasure of all—the very thing that all men need—then the most valuable gift God could give us is himself. This is one reason

God brings us trials—to help us learn our need for him. That is why God resists the proud, self-sufficient man, but gives grace to the humble man who seeks God (1 Peter 5:5). God is a rewarder of those who diligently seek him (Hebrews 11:6).

It's tempting to live a self-sufficient life in times of peace—when all is going well. But we don't need to wait for a trial to drive us to our knees. We can spend time in prayer talking with God. Talk to him about your day, your dreams and desires, and of course, your trials. Ask him to reveal himself to you in greater ways and increase your love for him. "Delight yourself in the LORD, and he will give you the desires of your heart" (Psalm 37:4). While our flesh might try to convince us otherwise, God is the ultimate desire of our hearts.

Self-sufficiency can often keep us from praying. We know we should pray, but we are so busy working out the challenges we face that we don't have time to pray. Or things seem to be working out fine. Why pray when all is going well? Too often, we forget that God is sovereign over all our lives, and we need his grace, strength, mercy, and favor.

For the man who learns to trust God in peacetime, nothing changes in battle. The Lord has him in the palm of his hands. When the bullets and grenades showered down on Desmond Doss, he didn't suddenly discover God; he called out to the loving Father he knew day by day to ask, "Lord, please help me get one more."

Today, we celebrate the heroism of Desmond Doss. Every time his story is told, God gets the glory. Let your life be a similar lens through which God's glory shines.

Get Started

Take time today to meditate on 1 John 5:14: "And this is the confidence that we have toward him, that if we ask anything according to his will he hears us."

Memorize the Lord's Prayer (Matthew 6:9–13), committing to memory one verse per day for five days. Take ten minutes during the day to pray according to the verse you are memorizing. Then pray that way each week for one month. Draw encouragement from the truth that God expects us to pray and ask for his help!

Take the Challenge

After completing the exercise above, memorize Psalm 73:25–28 and make Asaph's desires your desires. Ask God to help you make him the greatest desire of your life and your highest pursuit. You'll know when you're growing in your love for God because you will want to tell others about him.

4

Men Serve

"The greatest among you shall be your servant."
(Matthew 23:11)

The Super Bowl is a battle. It may not be an armed conflict, but with offense against defense and two quarterbacks on the attack against one another, it's one entertaining war. Upward of 100 million people tune in to watch opposing teams line up toe to toe on the gridiron battlefield. After the game clock expires and a champion is crowned, the Most Valuable Player is announced. On February 4, 2018, one of the most unlikely players received the award—Nick Foles, the backup quarterback for the Philadelphia Eagles. Foles took his team to victory through the end of the season, the playoffs, and ultimately the championship after the starting quarterback, Carson Wentz, blew out his knee with a handful of games to go.

Foles's road to victory wasn't easy. Though he saw success early in his career, his inconsistent performance on the field cost him a starting role more than once. Injuries didn't help. As Foles bounced from team to team, he struggled to accept the fact that God placed him in a role to serve as a backup, rather than a starter. As a result, he lost his love of the game. Foles likened the battle in his heart to a war. Who was he going to serve, himself or God?

After signing with the Eagles as Carson's backup, Foles took on the role as the team barista and made coffee for his teammates each morning to keep his "pride in check."[1] It reminded him that his role on the team was that of a servant, not a starter. Once Foles accepted the role of backup and purposed to do all things for glory to God and not his own glory, his joy and love for football returned. Foles gave his all to the backup role under Carson Wentz, the starter. He needed to study, practice, and stay fit, even though he might never enter a game. A backup must be ever ready to step in should the starting quarterback go down—and that was exactly what Nick did, taking his team all the way to the Super Bowl. "One of my favorite verses," Nick said, reflecting on his service to the team, "is Mark 10:45: 'The Son of Man came not to be served but to serve others.'"[2]

Jesus was the ultimate example of servanthood, and his example gives us both the model and motivation to lay down our lives in big and small ways. In a world that prizes competition and getting ahead, consider these words: "whoever would be great among you must be your servant, and whoever would be first among you must be your slave, even as the Son of Man came not to be served but to serve, and to give his life as a ransom for many" (Matthew 20:26–28).

So how would you evaluate your level of servanthood at work, home, or church? How do you respond to a call for men to stay late and help put tables away after a church event? Do you take your dishes into the kitchen after a meal, or do you expect others to serve you? How quick are you to give yourself up to serve your wife (Ephesians 5:25)? Are you eager to take on responsibilities at home that aren't typically yours? When someone asks for volunteers to help them load a moving truck, are you the first to raise your hand? All men want to do great things with their lives, but far fewer see service as the pathway. Yet Jesus could not have been clearer: those men who aspire to greatness must become servants.

Reflecting on his post-championship future, Nick Foles wrote,

"In the fifty-two-year history of the Super Bowl, there has never been another quarterback who has won the Super Bowl MVP and then started the next season on the bench. Until me. . . . To cheerfully return to a backup role after reaching the pinnacle of the sport contradicts everything the world tells us about success, fame, money, and self-worth. To me, it's a tangible reminder that we are called to humility and to a life of service."[3]

Get Started

Take time today to meditate on 1 Corinthians 10:31: "So, whether you eat or drink, or whatever you do, do all to the glory of God."

Are there any areas of your life where you are living for your own glory instead of living for the glory of God? Are there any areas of service you pass over because they are "beneath you"? Look for someone you can volunteer to serve in order to keep your focus on servanthood for the glory of God.

Take the Challenge

It is easy to serve at one-time events. It takes a much deeper commitment for regular service in your community or church. Prayerfully consider your level of service, and ask yourself, *If I truly believed that servanthood was the pathway to true greatness, what service teams could I join?* Service is often behind the scenes and goes unrecognized. Consider three ways you can serve others secretly—without announcing your service.

5

Men Follow the Spirit

"For all who are led by the Spirit of God are sons of God.
For you did not receive the spirit of slavery to fall back into
fear, but you have received the Spirit of adoption as sons, by
whom we cry, 'Abba! Father!'" (Romans 8:14–15)

Before a group of new recruits is trusted with a rifle and bullets, they learn to march. The name *drill sergeant* comes from their labors drilling their recruits on the parade field, turning a gaggle of city boys into a single cohesive marching unit. They march them back and forth until they dream, "Left . . . left, right, left." Cadets learn quickly that if you don't keep in step with the drill sergeant and the rest of your platoon, you create a tripping hazard. When your stride is out of sync, you end up stepping on the guy in front of you or you get stepped on from behind.

The drill sergeant marches alongside his soldiers, calling out the cadence and watching the way forward on behalf of his recruits. Commands are issued in advance of obstacles to keep a platoon from marching into a wall or other hazard. As long as you listen to the drill instructor and follow his lead, you will always reach your destination, though at times you may be marching to war.

The apostle Paul used this imagery in his exhortation to the Galatians when he said,

> But I say, walk by the Spirit, and you will not gratify
> the desires of the flesh. For the desires of the flesh

are against the Spirit, and the desires of the Spirit are against the flesh, for these are opposed to each other, to keep you from doing the things you want to do. But if you are led by the Spirit, you are not under the law. (5:16–18)

And those who belong to Christ Jesus have crucified the flesh with its passions and desires. If we live by the Spirit, let us also walk by the Spirit. Let us not become conceited, provoking one another, envying one another. (5:24–26)

God gave us his Holy Spirit to guide us day to day in our Christian walk. We, like the soldiers listening for the next marching command, need to hear what the Spirit of God is saying. The Spirit will speak to us. He reminds us of what we have learned from the Word (John 14:26). But we have to listen to his direction and say no to going our own way. Our sinful natures are drawn by the cravings of the world, rather than living for Christ. Sin is simply going our own way against the direction of the Spirit of God.

Imagine a platoon of soldiers with each member deciding where to go based on his or her own desires. It takes but a minute for a well-ordered platoon to devolve into chaos if they don't keep in step.

Like a soldier must learn to listen for a sergeant's drill commands, a believer must learn to hear the voice of the Spirit of God speaking through the Word of God. The Spirit of God is our helper (John16:7) who was sent to convict us when we sin (John 16:8). The Spirit is our assurance of salvation (Ephesians 1:17–20) and our guarantee of eternal life (Ephesians 1:13).

Mature men keep in step with the Spirit.

Get Started

Take time today to meditate on Psalm 143:10: "Teach me to do your will, for you are my God! Let your good Spirit lead me on level ground!"

Read your Bible prayerfully, asking the Spirit of God to help you learn. Then as you go about your day, invite the Spirit of God to speak to you and lead you. If we are commanded to keep in step and walk with the Spirit, we must be able to hear and know his voice. The Spirit of God will help you apply the Word. For instance, you may memorize a Bible verse such as "encourage one another" from 1 Thessalonians 5:11, but it is the Spirit who can prompt you to encourage a particular friend.

Take the Challenge

Identify three commands or encouragements from the Word of God that you believe the Spirit of God is calling you to apply to your life. Memorize those passages from Scripture and then daily ask the Spirit of God to help you apply them in your life. When those three are well ingrained in your memory, learn three more. That is how a drill sergeant teaches his platoon—a few commands at a time until they learn to understand the full counsel of his will. Likewise, you can learn to recognize the voice of the Spirit of God.

6

Men Are Responsible

"So then each of us will give an account of himself to God."
(Romans 14:12)

Lorenzo, my foxhole partner on a three-day war-game exercise, approached me with a panicked look on his face. "I can't find my M-16," he said. The one thing every soldier gets drilled into their head more than any other is "Don't lose your weapon." I can still hear Sergeant Harris shouting, "You are married to your weapon. You dress with it, you shower with it, and you go to bed with it at night, holding it tight." Lorenzo told me that he thought he set his M-16 down next to a tree during our daylong land navigation course the day before. "Oh, and one other thing," Lorenzo added. "I can't find my gas mask either." Knowing these were the two most essential pieces of equipment a soldier carried, I slowly backed away like he was infected with the plague. As I did, I gave him this advice: "you had better tell the drill sergeant." Then I waited for all you-know-what to break loose.

As men we're called to take responsibility for the gifts, talents, and wealth God has given us. Lorenzo provided a helpful refresher on this truth for our entire battalion, as all eight hundred of us trudged through the forest side by side. Four hours later, we abruptly returned to camp when Lorenzo "remembered" that he may have buried them that morning when he refilled the foxhole.

In the parable of the talents, a landowner going on a journey entrusted his property to three of his servants. Then he left. While he was gone, two of the three doubled the amounts they were given. The third servant buried his in the ground. (If only Lorenzo had known this parable, we might have avoided the exhausting search, which came minutes before we were about to load the trucks to mark the end of our three days in the field.)

When the master returned, he called his servants to account. He commended the men who demonstrated responsibility, but he condemned the man who did not, saying,

> "You wicked and slothful servant! You knew that I reap where I have not sown and gather where I scattered no seed? Then you ought to have invested my money with the bankers, and at my coming I should have received what was my own with interest. So take the talent from him and give it to him who has the ten talents. For to everyone who has will more be given, and he will have an abundance. But from the one who has not, even what he has will be taken away" (Matthew 25:26–29).

God entrusts each of us with talents and calls us to invest what we've been given toward the mission of the gospel. Husbands are called to love their wives. Fathers are called to disciple their children. We are called to give to the church, serve in the kingdom, and use our gifts and talents for the glory of God. We must not squander this responsibility by wasting time, procrastinating, or forgetting what is important—all of which is like burying our talent in the ground. True Christians live in service to their Master.

We found Lorenzo's M-16 and gas mask at the bottom of the foxhole that I had single-handedly dug three days before.

Lorenzo, who should have been taking turns in the digging, fell asleep in his forward observation position. So when it came time to fill in our hole, early that morning, he had to do it alone.

Once uncovered, Lorenzo's dirt-laden M-16 was surrendered to the drill sergeant. Every officer up the chain of command breathed a sigh of relief, for they each would have been held responsible for losing a weapon under their command. And we all learned a valuable lesson that day: take responsibility for the treasures you are given and never bury them in the ground.

Get Started

Take time today to meditate on Galatians 6:4–5: "Each one should test their own actions. Then they can take pride in themselves alone, without comparing themselves to someone else, for each one should carry their own load" (NIV).

Make a list of all your responsibilities and rate yourself on a scale of 1 to 10, 1 being unfaithful and 10 being extremely faithful. Then ask yourself the question, what can I do to advance one of these responsibilities toward greater faithfulness? Choose one way and come up with a plan. That could mean cleaning off the desk your boss asked you to clear weeks ago. Or painting the trim you promised your wife you would complete, getting your oil changed, or starting family devotions again.

Take the Challenge

Working from your list in the Get Started section, purpose to take another small step to grow in faithfulness in your responsibilities during each of the next thirty days. Taking consistent small steps and initiatives can help you climb a mountain. At the end of thirty days, reevaluate your life. You will marvel at the measure of accomplishment that a lifestyle of regular faithful living can produce.

7

Men Keep Their Word

"When a man makes a vow to the LORD or takes an oath
to obligate himself by a pledge, he must not break his word
but must do everything he said." (Numbers 30:2 NIV)

The Battle of Helm's Deep is one of the greatest fictional war battles of all time. In the movie version, *The Lord of the Rings: The Two Towers*, a massive Uruk-hai orc army marches against the fortress. Knowing they can't defend the burg without more soldiers, Gandalf departs Aragorn to search for reinforcements from the horseman of Rohan. He leaves Aragorn with these words: "Look to my coming, at first light, on the fifth day. At dawn, look to the East." Five days later, when the fortress is falling, as the first light of the morning sun bursts through a parapet window, Aragorn remembers Gandalf's promise. Moments later, Aragorn and King Theoden make their final charge against the Uruk-hai. Gandalf returns as promised, on a white horse along with the entire Rohirrim army. With the blazing morning sun beaming at their backs, the army blinds their enemy and the orcs are defeated. Gandalf kept his word.

There is an old saying, "A man's word is his bond." When Aragorn remembered Gandalf's words on the fifth day, he charged into the battle with confidence that those words could be trusted. A man's faithfulness to his word is a measure of his manhood. James repeats a command first given by Jesus (Matthew 5:37) when he says, "let your 'yes' be yes and your 'no' be no" (James 5:12). Jesus modeled the faithfulness he calls all men to keep.

Jesus kept his word, and by it, we were saved. He told the disciples, "The Son of Man must suffer many things and be rejected by the elders and chief priests and scribes, and be killed, and on the third day be raised" (Luke 9:22). While in the garden, just before his arrest, Jesus prayed that his Father would, "Remove this cup." Still, Jesus did not rescind his offer to give up his life for our sins, for he added, "Nevertheless, not my will, but yours, be done" (Luke 22:42). The Father did not take the cup from his Son, so Jesus did not resist when the soldiers came to arrest him. Jesus kept his word and will keep it again and return one day to restore the earth.

Gandalf's return on a white horse with the blinding sun behind him seems borrowed from the book of Revelation. John describes the scene of his vision this way:

> Then I saw heaven opened, and behold, a white horse! The one sitting on it is called Faithful and True, and in righteousness he judges and makes war. His eyes are like a flame of fire, and on his head are many diadems, and he has a name written that no one knows but himself. He is clothed in a robe dipped in blood, and the name by which he is called is The Word of God. (Revelation 19:11–13)

The book of Revelation precedes Christ's promise to return soon with this exhortation: "These words are trustworthy and true" (22:6). The words of Revelation are trustworthy and true because Jesus is "Faithful and True." His yes is yes.

So, what about you? Are your words trustworthy and true? When you say you will do something, do you follow through? Do you keep your promises? It is said in another adage, "A man's word is worth his weight in gold." It would take a man's entire life wages to purchase his weight in gold. That is how valuable your promise is.

Get Started

Take time today to meditate on Proverbs 25:14 (NLT): "A person who promises a gift but doesn't give it is like clouds and wind that bring no rain."

Think over the last few years of your life. Have you made any commitments or promises that you have yet to fulfill? If so, look to complete that to which you have given your word. If you've promised to lend a hand to a brother, schedule a time to help him. If you've promised to take your wife on a date, take your daughter to the beach, or complete a task at work, make sure your yes is yes and complete those tasks. Watch what you say today to ensure that you make no empty promises. Consider asking for forgiveness from people affected by your failure to keep your commitments, and then purpose to live differently.

Take the Challenge

Once you have completed the above assignment, use your phone to record promises you make. Review your promises daily for an extended period—that could be a month or even a year, however long it takes you to become more aware of the promises you make. The goal is to learn to only pledge to do what you purpose to complete. By becoming faithful to your promises and commitments, you will become a man of your word, faithful and true.

Read and think about Proverbs 25:14 (NLT): "A person who promises a gift but doesn't give it is like clouds and wind that bring no rain."

8

Men Stay on Mission

"Go into all the world and proclaim the gospel
to the whole creation." (Mark 16:15)

What would you do if you found yourself facing a battalion of more than thirty enemy machine gunners, raking the bushes with bullets above your head?

That is the exact situation Corporal Alvin York met on the morning of October 8, 1918. His squad was given the mission to take out a German machine gun position. The squad circled around and made it behind enemy lines. As they crept back toward the machine gunners, they surprised a German field meeting and captured thirty enemy soldiers. Moments later, when the machine gunners realized what was going on behind them, they turned around and opened fire, not more than forty yards ahead. Nine Americans were shot, including the sergeant in command. This left Corporal York in charge, with seven privates all pinned down in a gully and dozens of machine gunners firing hundreds of rounds at their position.

York, an expert marksman, didn't lose sight of the mission to neutralize the machine guns. One by one, Alvin took out the enemy soldiers until the unit surrendered. When the smoke cleared, twenty-eight German machine gun battalion soldiers were dead, one for each of the bullets York fired. The official U.S. Army record reads, "Practically unassisted, he [York] captured

132 Germans, took about 35 machine guns, and killed no less than 25 of the enemy."[1]

Remaining focused on your primary mission will keep you in the fight when the bullets of life start to fly. So what is our primary mission as believers? For starters, we follow our Captain, Jesus, and his mission. Jesus articulated the mission with this phrase: "I will build my church, and the gates of hell shall not prevail against it" (Matthew 16:18). Just before returning to heaven, Jesus gave the Great Commission: "All authority in heaven and on earth has been given to me. Go therefore and make disciples of all nations, baptizing them in the name of the Father and of the Son and of the Holy Spirit, teaching them to observe all that I have commanded you. And behold, I am with you always, to the end of the age" (Matthew 28:18–20).

With those two statements, Jesus gave every Christian marching orders. If you're a believer, your primary mission is to spread the gospel and make disciples—disciples of your wife, children, friends, and neighbors. The gospel is the saving truth that Jesus, who knew no sin, took on our sin and died on the cross in our place, that those who believe can be forgiven. Then Jesus rose from the grave on the third day, proving his victory over sin and death. It is this life-saving message that we are called to share. As for making disciples, that is best done within the context of service in a local church.

It seems like a simple mission, yet life is full of opportunities and trials that distract us and occupy our time. Those who remain mission-focused can take advantage of the day-to-day interactions we have with people who need the truth we've been entrusted to share. No matter what is happening around you, your mission is clear—share the gospel message and build the church. We can't be too busy, too tired, or too afraid, even if life's trials, like bullets over our heads, have us pinned down.

Get Started

Take time today to meditate on Hebrews 10:38: "But my righteous one shall live by faith, and if he shrinks back, my soul has no pleasure in him. But we are not of those who shrink back and are destroyed, but of those who have faith and preserve their souls." How would you evaluate your faith? Are you trusting in Jesus for your salvation? Jesus died on the cross for our sins and calls all of us to turn from our sins, trust him in faith, and live our lives in service to him.

The first step to living for Christ is connecting to a local church. If you are not a committed member of a local church, plan to get involved with one. Then read through some of the key gospel passages and pray for opportunities to share your faith with others. Study Matthew 28:18–20; Romans 10:14–17; and 1 Corinthians 2:1–5.

Take the Challenge

Make an honest list of your life's priorities. Where does Christ's mission to build the church and our command to share the gospel fit into your priorities? How would your life need to change to move those closer to the top of your priorities? What would you need to change to place it at the very top? Evaluate your practical commitment to Christ's mission by considering the following two key areas: What is your commitment to sharing the gospel? What is the level of your attendance, service, and giving in your local church? Share your evaluation and determination to press in with another believer who can hold you accountable to grow in this area.

9

Men Read

"Your word is a lamp to my feet and a light to my path."
(Psalm 119:105)

Josiah became king when he was eight years old, during a time when Israel served idols and had forgotten God's Word. Josiah ordered the restoration of God's temple and during that work, the Book of the Law was found—likely the Torah, the first five books of the Bible. When the words of the Law were read to Josiah, he tore his clothes in repentance for the sins of the nation. Josiah sought the Lord and then knew exactly what had to be done—he had to read the book to the entire nation.

So Josiah commanded that all Israel be assembled at the temple, from the least to the greatest, and there the king read to them "all the words of the Book of the Covenant, which had been found in the Temple of the Lord" (2 Kings 23:2 NIV). There, before all the people, Josiah pledged to obey the Lord by keeping all his commands, laws, and decrees with all his heart and soul (2 Kings 23:3). Josiah knew the only way to unlock the wisdom of God's Word was to read it.

When asked to share the key to success in life, the great investor Warren Buffet pointed to a shelf of books and said, "Read 500 pages like this every day. That's how knowledge works. It builds up, like compound interest. All of you can do it, but I guarantee not many of you will do it."[1] While five hundred pages is beyond most of us, reading just thirty minutes a day can transform your life, especially if ten minutes of that thirty is reading

God's Word. For every minute of reading per day, you can read a book per year. So if you read twenty minutes a day, you'll read twenty books in a year. And by reading the Bible for ten minutes a day, you will read through the Bible in one year.

If you are one of the guys who put forward the objection "I'm not a reader," here is a word of advice from Sergeant Harris: "Drop that sorry excuse right now." Given that God calls us to study and meditate on the Word of God (Psalm 1:2) and it is the power of God for our salvation (Romans 1:16), we were all created to hear God in his Word. Reading is one of the best ways to accomplish that!

Words are the currency of wisdom, and God created them so that we might gain the greatest treasure—Christ. Consider what Paul wrote to the young Timothy:

> But as for you, continue in what you have learned and have firmly believed, knowing from whom you learned it and how from childhood you have been acquainted with the sacred writings, which are able to make you wise for salvation through faith in Christ Jesus. All Scripture is breathed out by God and profitable for teaching, for reproof, for correction, and for training in righteousness, that the man of God may be competent, equipped for every good work. (2 Timothy 3:14–17)

Now that you know you're called to read, it's time to apply this lesson to your life. If you read and walk away without application, you won't change. But when you apply what you read, you can change. The goal is to renew your mind. Paul wrote, "Do not be conformed to this world, but be transformed by the renewal of your mind, that by testing you may discern what is the will of God, what is good and acceptable and perfect" (Romans 12:2).

Get Started

Take time today to meditate on Paul's request of Timothy in 2 Timothy 4:13: "When you come, bring the cloak that I left with Carpus at Troas, also the books, and above all the parchments."

Finish this book, reading one devotion each day, and also read one chapter from the Gospel of Matthew each day. Start asking your friends for suggestions of the best books they have read. Hearing their excitement will stir your own. Make a list of the suggested books you want to read. Follow book recommendations from Christian publications like *Christianity Today*, The Gospel Coalition, and Tim Challies's website.[2]

Take the Challenge

In addition to finishing this book, take the thirty-minutes-a-day reading challenge. Read the Bible for ten minutes a day and a book of your choice for twenty. When you finish that book, take up another from your list. Don't allow yourself screen time if you miss a day; no TV, Facebook on smartphones, or video games.

10

Men Slay Sloth

"The soul of the sluggard craves and gets nothing, while the soul of the diligent is richly supplied." (Proverbs 13:4)

Solomon challenged his sons to be like the ant: "Go to the ant, O sluggard; consider her ways, and be wise. Without having any chief, officer, or ruler, she prepares her bread in summer and gathers her food in harvest" (Proverbs 6:6–8). The ant, Solomon taught his sons, gets to work on time, doesn't have to be told to work hard, and doesn't eat all the harvest. What about you? Do you arrive and get started on time? Do you take the initiative to work without being told? Do you save for future needs that are sure to come?

Between August of 1915 and June of 1917, thousands of British soldiers worked like ants, around the clock, digging under the German army's position in Messines, Belgium. In total, the Royal Engineer Tunneling Companies excavated more than twenty deep tunnels and caverns. Those caverns were filled with close to a million pounds of explosives. The Allied commanders tricked their German counterparts by staging a series of smaller attacks through tunnels they had dug above the forty-foot-deep main offensive. "They even rigged up picks and shovels to scrape at the ground remotely by pulling a string, so that the Germans would blow up unoccupied tunnels."[1]

The Germans suspected the British might be digging deeper, and they set out listening posts to catch any sound of shovel or pick against a rock. Two years after the digging began, on June 7, 1917, the Allies detonated the explosives. The blast, the loudest non-nuclear explosion of all time, could be heard as far away as London.[2] The coordinated offensive is considered one of the most successful offensives of WWI. It was made possible as the direct result of the tireless hard work of Allied soldiers who did not give up for fear of dying. As Solomon said, "The sluggard says, 'There is a lion outside! I shall be killed in the streets!'" (Proverbs 22:13).

Sloth tells you that you don't have to do anything that you are not forced to do. Sloth believes it is somebody else's job to work hard; you only need to do what is necessary to afford time to rest. The sluggard never saves for the future; he expects a helping hand. The sluggard can barely take care of himself, let alone take responsibility for a family. What makes sloth so dangerous is that there is no horrible crime to avoid; you simply decide to take a minute to rest—again and again.

Sloth can set in when unbelief and discouragement take the reins in our hearts. We don't try because we think we will just fail the next day. Examine your heart. What lies do you believe that lead to fear or unbelief and empower sloth? The greatest tasks all begin with working at the problem for ten minutes. Trust the Lord to work through you. The moment you trust God and give ten minutes of work toward your problem you have reversed course and have gone from wasting time to work.

Paul told Timothy, "if anyone does not provide for his relatives, and especially for members of his household, he has denied the faith and is worse than an unbeliever" (1 Timothy 5:8). It's also important to say that a man's work doesn't end when he punches the clock to leave the office. The moment a husband or father walks through the front door he starts his most important job—leading the family. We need to say no to the easy chair.

It's important to rest from our labors, to gain the strength we need to work hard again. But for the sluggard, tomorrow never becomes a day for work. A little slumber seems harmless at first, but if left unchecked, sloth can rob a man blind. Solomon said it this way, "A little sleep, a little slumber, a little folding of the hands to rest, and poverty will come upon you like a robber, and want like an armed man" (Proverbs 6:10–11).

We are all called by God to work for the good of others. Sloth would have us forget about God's call to labor and think only of ourselves. Labor is a fundamental component of our identity and is a call God places over all of us. If you are wondering what you should do for work, start with the needs you see around you. Folks welcome those who offer to fill a need.

Get Started

Take time today to meditate on 2 Thessalonians 3:10: "For even when we were with you, we would give you this command: If anyone is not willing to work, let him not eat."

Where is sloth most likely to rob you? Ask the Holy Spirit to show you one thing you can do to reverse the effects of sloth in your life. What has been on your to-do list for the most extended amount of time? Consider what one thing you could do to combat sloth in your life and then purpose to let nothing stop you from completing that task. Secondly, commit to arriving early for an appointment you usually arrive late for.

Take the Challenge

Doing what we are told, on time, can keep sloth at bay, but nothing deals a death blow to sloth more than taking the initiative to do more. Make a list of ten ways you could take the initiative at work, church, or home. Then schedule those tasks into your free time. Share your list with someone who can hold you accountable to accomplish the tasks you set out to do.

11

Men Know Their Enemy

"Be sober-minded; be watchful. Your adversary the devil prowls around like a roaring lion, seeking someone to devour." (1 Peter 5:8)

The Art of War by Sun Tzu is considered one of the greatest books of battle stratagem ever written. While the book is a compendium of offensive strategies, it can also serve to help you understand how and where your enemy will attack. If you flip Tzu's insights around, they can help you prepare your defenses. For example, Tzu says to attack your enemy where he's weak. Well, that is exactly where your enemy will attack you. So shore up your weaknesses. Sun Tzu directs an army to pretend to be weak and then attack. Your enemy may also pretend to be vulnerable. Then, when he sees you let down your guard, he goes on the attack. Your adversary will want you to think he is far away when he is near and nearby when he is far. An adversary will attack where you least expect because "all warfare is based on deception."[1] Be glad that you'll never meet Sun Tzu on the battlefield.

But these cunning strategies don't find their origin in Sun Tzu. They're based on the age-old operation of the devil, our enemy, the one the Bible calls "the deceiver of the whole world" (Revelation 12:9) and "the father of lies" (John 8:44). Satan, like Sun Tzu, will make you think he is far away when he is about to attack and hit you where you least expect it and are most unprepared for it.

Peter offers us this advice, "Be sober-minded; be watchful. Your adversary the devil prowls around like a roaring lion, seeking someone to devour" (1 Peter 5:8). Peter knew well the wiles of the enemy. Just before the crucifixion, Jesus warned Simon Peter, who underestimated the power of the enemy to exploit his own weakness. Peter thought of himself as a capable soldier, ready to fight alongside Jesus. But battle rarely unfolds as smoothly as we think. Consider Jesus's warning and Peter's confident reply.

> "Simon, Simon, behold, Satan demanded to have you, that he might sift you like wheat, but I have prayed for you that your faith may not fail. And when you have turned again, strengthen your brothers." Peter said to him, "Lord, I am ready to go with you both to prison and to death." Jesus said, "I tell you, Peter, the rooster will not crow this day, until you deny three times that you know me." (Luke 22:31–34)

None of us can afford to be so self-confident that we let our guard down. Few men plan to embezzle money, cheat on their wives, or abuse drugs, but the enemy takes men out with these temptations every day. Often it is the little compromises we make that lead to the bigger sins. Brian Hedges in an article on watchfulness said,

> "The discipline of watching is like a home security system. An effective surveillance system includes several components, such as security cameras, motion sensors, floodlights, electric locks, and high-decibel alarms. All these components serve one purpose: protecting the home from dangerous intruders. In similar

fashion, watchfulness embraces a variety of practices, such as self-examination, prayer, meditation, and accountability, but all governed by the single intention of keeping the heart."[2]

Don't be like Peter, who underestimated his enemy and suffered from self-confidence. No one makes fun of a soldier in battle who digs in for the fight. When the battle comes, the soldier who worked all night to pile rocks in front of his foxhole is less likely to get picked off. So what are you waiting for? Start digging because the attack comes before dawn.

Get Started

Take time today to meditate on Ephesians 6:11–12: "Put on the whole armor of God, that you may be able to stand against the schemes of the devil. For we do not wrestle against flesh and blood, but against the rulers, against the authorities, against the cosmic powers over this present darkness, against the spiritual forces of evil in the heavenly places."

Your enemy the devil is looking for ways to attack you. He's seen your weaknesses. You don't think he is watching, but he is. Where have you failed in the past? The enemy knows your history. How might he attack you again? For example, you may be inclined to watch inappropriate shows when alone on business trips. Make a list of the ways you are vulnerable to temptation, given your past history with sin. Then draw near to Christ and remember that he has given you his Spirit to help you in your weakness (2 Corinthians 12:9–10). Be wiser than your enemy. Next to each area of weakness list at least one practical step that you can take to prevent yourself from falling into that temptation.

Take the Challenge

There is wisdom behind the army's practice of assigning two men in every foxhole. While one guards the front line, the other sleeps. Similarly, there is no substitute for an accountability partner. Share the list you completed in the Get Started exercise with another guy who is willing to join you in your battle against the enemy. Discuss the various ways the enemy might try to tempt either of you to let down your guard. Meet weekly for a month and then monthly for a year.

12

Men Attack Their Problems

"The wicked flee when no one pursues, but the righteous
are bold as a lion." (Proverbs 28:1)

Just after taking over command of Israel, Joshua stood outside the promised land with the Jordan River at flood stage
and flowing between him and Canaan. Imagine him standing
in front of what looked like an impenetrable river and realizing
that, once through the river, well-fortified cities with vast armies
stood against him. Moses, the guy who led them out of Egypt,
was dead. Now he was left in charge. The way forward seemed
impossible.

If his people weren't swept away by the current, many would
be cut down in the battle. What do you think he might have felt?
As you can imagine, Joshua was afraid. But God didn't leave
him in that place alone. God spoke to Joshua to encourage him
to advance, saying, "Obey my law and go over this Jordan." In
other words, trust God and advance. You've got a job to do. And
he gave Joshua this advice: "Be strong and courageous. Do not
be frightened, and do not be dismayed, for the LORD your God
is with you wherever you go" (Joshua 1:9). Now that is some
good advice that we can all take into our daily battles. So much
of life would come easier if we simply believed that "if God is for
us, who can be against us? He who did not spare his own Son but
gave him up for us all, how will he not also with him graciously
give us all things?" (Romans 8:31–32).

Too often we avoid a difficult situation rather than press into it with faith. We are afraid to talk to someone about a difficult relationship, to raise questions that our boss might not welcome, to ask for a raise, to confront sin in a friend's life, or to tell the truth and confess our own sin. Rather than study for that certification and take the test or apply for the job posting that would give us a promotion, we shrink back—even when we have a sense that it is something we should do. What relationship, emotional, and spiritual challenges are you facing that feel like the Jordan River at flood stage or a fortified city that seems unconquerable?

God opened the way for Joshua by holding back the Jordan so that all of Israel could cross on dry ground (Joshua 3:16–17). When the armies of Canaan heard what God did in drying up the Jordan, their "hearts melted" with fear. Then the Son of God showed up as the commander of God's army to call them to advance on the fortified city of Jericho. When Israel obeyed, the imposing walls came down with a shout and a trumpet blast (Joshua 6:20).

Take a moment to assess yourself on this issue. Where are you giving in to temptation to fear or worry, rather than trusting God and advancing? Does fear keep you from taking the initiative at work or repairing that broken relationship? Does fear keep you from sharing your faith? In all these things, remember that the Lord has your back. If you sense the Lord is calling you to action, and the work ahead is good and righteous, then take a step of faith. Put your foot forward into the water and watch God work to part the waters he has called you to cross.

Get Started

Take time today to meditate on Romans 8:31–32: "If God is for us, who can be against us? He who did not spare his own Son but gave him up for us all, how will he not also with him graciously give us all things?"

God has called us to attack our problems, not shrink back in fear. And he has promised if we come to him that he'll help us. Where are you giving in to fear and worry in your life? Make a list and then—after asking for God's help—go after the most significant temptation in your life.

Take the Challenge

When it comes to fear and worry, it's best to go on the counter-attack. If you're struggling to find time to exercise, don't just try to remember to go to the gym in the morning. Take the offensive; sign up for a 5K and train. If you are weak at memorizing Scripture, don't just try to memorize a verse; work on memorizing a whole chapter. It can also help to share your struggles with another believer and ask him for help in the fight. His prayers and counsel can help you keep your courage to follow through.

13

Men Honor Women

"Charm is deceitful, and beauty is vain, but a woman who fears the LORD is to be praised." (Proverbs 31:30)

Back in the early 1980s, when I entered the service, the US Army experimented with coed basic training. I can remember my first days standing to attention on the parade field alongside at least a dozen women in my platoon. At first, I wondered how they would hold up, but I soon discovered that many of the women were tougher than I was. They scored high on tests and were equally capable marksman. They were unafraid of heights, compared to some of the guys who melted at the thought of descending "Australian style" (face-first) down the rappelling tower.

They, like all of us guys, made mistakes. But the drill sergeants didn't mock them mercilessly like they did the men. I'm not sure how male drill sergeants relate today, but back then, every one of our drill sergeants (who were all men) had a line they would not cross. They wanted to ensure the female recruits were prepared to be soldiers, but they were careful not to degrade them, something they were all too happy to do to the guys. While berating us guys when we failed, they honored the women by encouraging them.

This is particularly relevant to the way men treat their wives. Peter wrote, "Likewise, husbands, live with your wives in an understanding way, showing honor to the woman as the weaker vessel, since they are heirs with you of the grace of life, so that your prayers may not be hindered" (1 Peter 3:7). Peter addresses husbands in this verse, but his words extend beyond marriage and can be applied to the way men should treat all women. Single men who learn to treat women with honor gain practical training for marriage and honoring their wife later on.

Peter's short exhortation communicates two essential principles. First, women are equal in worth. They're fellow heirs of God's grace and salvation. They, like men, are made in the image of God, equal in worth with men. But that doesn't make them identical to men. The reason Peter gives for his command to show honor and understanding toward wives is because women are the "weaker vessel." So, while women were created with equal worth, they're different from men in function. Although today's culture is tossing out fundamental truths about gender, my drill sergeants seemed to know that women should be honored. Paul directs men to treat all women with honor in his exhortation to Timothy. He writes, treat the "older women as mothers, younger women as sisters, in all purity" (1 Timothy 5:2).

Physically, most men are taller and stronger than most women. Functionally, God calls men to lead in their marriage (1 Corinthians 11:3; Ephesians 5:23) and sacrifice for their wives (Ephesians 5:25). Women are called to submit to and honor their spouse and serve as a helper and partner with their husband (Genesis 2:18). God's design for these differing functions flourishes when men lead with understanding, remain faithful in their marriage, and treat their wives with honor as the weaker vessel. When men abandon these principles, it often results in broken marriages. Perhaps that is why God warns men that he will turn a deaf ear toward a man's prayers if he dishonors his wife.

Get Started

Take time today to meditate on the second half of 1 Timothy 5:1–2: "Do not rebuke an older man but encourage him as you would a father, younger men as brothers, older women as mothers, younger women as sisters, in all purity."

Look for ways you can honor the women in your life today. What are some ways you can demonstrate the principles found in Ephesians 5 and 1 Peter 3:7?

Take the Challenge

Memorize 1 Peter 3:7 and make a list of five ways you can demonstrate honor toward the women God has placed in your life. If you are single, consider whether you are well prepared to provide for a home or remain faithful in marriage. If you are married, how would your wife say you are doing at following the principles presented in this section? Imagine for a moment that she knows everything about you, what would she say? Share your answer to that question with your accountability partner.

14

Men Guard Their Eyes

"Everyone who looks at a woman with lustful intent
has already committed adultery with her in his heart."
(Matthew 5:28)

"**G**ive me your eyes!" Sergeant Harris shouted toward one of our guys as he reviewed the steps to take apart an M-16 rifle. It wasn't a request; it was a warning. Failing to pay attention could cost us our lives. Harris knew that the mind followed the eyes. If we were looking at him during his demonstration, we were less likely to be distracted by the female recruits in our unit. Harris knew guarding our eyes was the best way to avoid tempting distractions. A soldier's eyes are his best offensive weapon in battle, but they can be his greatest downfall when it comes to temptation.

Jesus said it like this, "The eye is the lamp of the body. So, if your eye is healthy, your whole body will be full of light, but if your eye is bad, your whole body will be full of darkness," (Matthew 6:22–23). Knowing how our eyes can lead our mind and soul astray, Job declared, "I have made a covenant with my eyes; how then could I gaze at a virgin?" (Job 31:1).

Harris taught us how to use the cans from our C-Rations, hung along a string to provide an early warning signal of the enemies' approach. And even more useful, he taught us how to set up a trip wire to a claymore mine far in advance of our lines. The principle was simple: set your defenses forward of your position.

Making a covenant with your eyes is a forward defense against sexual sin.

There are few temptations a man faces in life that are greater than lust, and there is no quicker way to lust than looking. Job understood the connection between his eyes and heart. He wrote of his eye pledge as a married man. Later Job further explained that when it comes to sexual temptation, your heart follows after your eyes (31:7), and soon your feet follow your heart (31:9).

As young men cross over into puberty and mature sexually, they need to learn how to steward this gift. God designed our sexual drive for a marriage relationship. But the sex drive is like a wild stallion in a corral, looking to break free. It doesn't want to be broken, bridled, and tethered to a wagon or saddled. However, once that stallion is broken, it learns the joy of pleasing its owner, and it enjoys a lifetime of faithful service. There is great joy in sexual expression within the protected bounds of a committed marriage. But marriage isn't a singular solution to lust. A man who doesn't control his eyes before marriage is not likely to find that discipline just because he wears a wedding band. And if he doesn't control his eyes, lust will not be far behind.

To make things even more challenging, Jesus said, "But I say to you that everyone who looks at a woman with lustful intent has already committed adultery with her in his heart" (Matthew 5:28). There is a fine line between appreciating the beautiful figure of a woman and undressing her in your mind, whether or not she is dressed in today's tight-fitting yoga pants or a skimpy bathing suit.

Follow Job's example and protect your heart by making a covenant with your eyes. Doing so will help ensure that your feet don't travel to another woman's door, which can be as close as the next swipe of your finger on the cell phone in your pocket. Like Sergeant Harris, Jesus calls us to keep our eyes fixed on him, the perfecter of our faith, the one who died for us (Hebrews 12:2). One practical discipline you can employ is to avoid taking a second look at women who capture your desire. Avoiding that second glance is the best way to guard your heart from lusting.

Get Started

Take time today to meditate on Psalm 119:37: "Turn my eyes from looking at worthless things; and give me life in your ways."

Write out a pledge to God that you will guard your eyes and go one week without a second look. Make a list of all the places you frequent where you are tempted to look lustfully at women and avoid those places while you walk out your pledge. If you are one of the many men whose playground is the cell phone in your pocket, disable the internet on your phone for that week and use it only as a phone.

Take the Challenge

Confess your failures to another Christian guy who can hold you accountable. Set up a regular accountability meeting. Don't give into the lie that you can handle this challenge on your own. God pours out a special grace upon the man who humbles himself and invites accountability (1 Peter 5:5–6). You can use an online surfing accountability tool like www.covenanteyes.com to provide you with screen accountability.

15

Men Demonstrate Fidelity

"Many a man proclaims his own steadfast love, but a
faithful man who can find?" (Proverbs 20:6)

I grew up in the age of vinyl records. Music recorded and replayed from plastic discs. Along with the music, you could
hear a hiss in the background. It was most noticeable before and
after every song. A scratch could also affect the record's fidelity,
causing the needle to make a skipping sound or jump groves and
repeat or skip ahead in a song. I can remember listening with my
college friends to digital music for the first time. The clarity of
the sound amazed us, but we were most astounded by the few
seconds of pristine silence between songs—no hiss! Again and
again we replayed the gaps, from the last note of the previous
song to the first of the next. The silence was beautiful, the music
amazing—pure faithfulness, music with perfect fidelity.

We don't use the word *fidelity* much today, but it's a beautiful word and a mandate for every man's life. We're called to be
men of fidelity, faithful to God and faithful to man. Fidelity is
a crucial component of a man's integrity. Perhaps that is why
the Marine Corps adopted "Semper Fidelis" (always faithful) as
their motto. A faithful man can tell a lie, but a man who lacks
faithfulness is a lie. Fidelity is measured by how closely a man's
practice matches his promise.

I saw fidelity in action in my father. He got up for work every
weekday, loved my mom through her last day of life, attended

church every Sunday, and lifted us kids up in regular prayer. Faithful is a description of my dad's character.

Sexual faithfulness in marriage is a unique measure of our fidelity as men. Since marriage is designed to portray the fidelity of God toward his children (Ephesians 5:32), sexual infidelity is a direct insult to God (Psalm 51:4). Fidelity requires that I love my wife exclusively (which compares to the music) and allow nothing to distort the music of my promise—no adultery, no pornography, no second glances (like the hiss and scratches). If you're a single man, you have no less responsibility to fidelity, which you'll one day promise your future bride. And as a single man, you have no less responsibility toward God. Sexual immorality is always adultery against God.

In addition to fidelity in marriage, fidelity is required in every relationship. When you accept a job, it comes with your promise to arrive on time, work during work hours, and not give company time to your smartphone. When you agree to help a friend, fidelity to that pledge means you follow through and keep your word. When you promise to attend your child's concert or game, fidelity demands that you don't allow excuses to prevent your attendance.

Most important of all is your fidelity toward God. He who created you demands it. "You shall have no other gods before me" (Exodus 20:3). While most don't bow at carved idols, we all divide our love for God with our pursuit of pleasure. We must love the Lord our God with all of our heart, soul, mind, and strength (Matthew 22:37; Mark 12:30). We're called to cut out the noise. Our fidelity, the degree to which we are faithful, is the greatest measure of our manhood. Real men keep their promises and live a life free of every scratch that might mar the fidelity of their word.

Few men finish well. Every man should live with hope of hearing the Lord speak the words, "Well done, good and faithful servant" (Matthew 25:21). I am certain those are the first words my father heard as he stepped away from this world into the presence of Jesus when he passed into glory. Too many men live for the pleasure of the moment and miss the greater lasting joy that comes from giving up a short-term sinful pleasure for God's eternal commendation. Remember, nothing impacts the next generation greater than a life lived faithful to a man's final breath.

Get Started

Take time today to meditate on 1 Corinthians 4:1–2: "This is how one should regard us, as servants of Christ and stewards of the mysteries of God. Moreover, it is required of stewards that they be found trustworthy."

Write a list of any areas where you have not been faithful. You can include small things like lacking faithfulness to follow through or not attending church. But you should also list any serious failings to remain faithful. Know that Jesus always has more than enough grace for your sin. Confess your failings to the Lord and prayerfully ask God to help you know what you can do to restore fidelity in each area.

Take the Challenge

Share your list with your pastor or a trusted, faithful friend, and ask them if they can advise you as to any action steps you should take. Enter into an accountability relationship with another man. Meet monthly for one year to encourage one another and hold each other accountable to live a faithful life in all things.

16

Men Tell the Truth

"Keep your tongue from evil and your lips
from speaking deceit." (Psalm 34:13)

In 2014, the United States Air Force relieved dozens of officers from their positions. They were dismissed as a result of an investigation that revealed upwards of one hundred junior officers cheated on exams. The scandal uncovered a widespread practice of officers texting answers to one another during monthly proficiency examinations. While the military assured the public that the country's nuclear readiness was never compromised, the scale of the cheating uncovered by the probe was unprecedented. The probe discovered "that a policy of '100 percent or fail' on the monthly proficiency exams resulted in unhealthy pressure from commanders and high anxiety among missile officers that contributed to the cheating."[1]

Two professors at the U.S. Army War College further explained how "ethical fading and rationalizing allow individuals to convince themselves that their honor and integrity are intact despite ethical compromise."[2] Simply put, when the pressure is on and everybody else is doing it, it is easy to lie. When keeping your integrity means failure, it's easy to justify cheating as the lesser evil.

What about you? Where are you tempted to shade the truth? Shading the truth sounds better than lying, doesn't it? Do you report all your income on your taxes? Do you confess that you forgot when your boss asks if the report is finished? Do you admit to eating the last of the ice cream when you hear the question coming from the kitchen, or do you fade back into your bedroom until the trouble passes? As long as you don't have to say anything, it's not lying to withhold your admission, right? It sounds like a bit of "ethical fading."

Just before his arrest, Jesus prayed to his Father for all who would one day believe in his name (John 17:20). What did he pray for? To help us know and tell the truth. Jesus prayed, "Sanctify them in the truth; your word is truth" (John 17:17). While man's sinful nature is bent toward self-protection and telling lies, the spirit of truth (John 16:13) is ever transforming us into the image of God, who cannot lie (Titus 1:2; Hebrews 6:18). When Jesus returns, he'll come with the name "Faithful and True" (Revelation 19:11) to rescue us from a world of lies. If you love our Lord Jesus, then live your new self in Christ; battle against lies and live with integrity as the man of truth God called you to be. The Spirit of truth will help you fight.

Scripture is clear about lying. David wrote, "Keep your tongue from evil and your lips from speaking deceit. Turn away from evil and do good; seek peace and pursue it. The eyes of the LORD are toward the righteous and his ears toward their cry. The face of the LORD is against those who do evil, to cut off the memory of them from the earth" (Psalm 34:13–16). Solomon followed with strong words against deceit: "The LORD detests lying lips, but he delights in people who are trustworthy" (Proverbs 12:22 NIV; cf. 13:5). Lying, in effect, nailed Jesus to the cross as he endured false accusations (see Mark 14:55–56). So how can we indulge in that which ultimately sent Jesus to the cross?

The next time you're tempted to try and top another guy's fish story with one of your own or make up a half-truth excuse for why a project isn't finished, just keep your mouth closed. Take a moment before you "stretch the truth" to remember the prayer

Jesus offered up moments before his arrest and crucifixion, and then live in the good of your salvation. For it was upon the cross that our sin of lying was nailed so that we could be forgiven and filled with the Spirit of truth and say no to every lie.

Get Started

Take time today to meditate on John 8:31–32: "So Jesus said to the Jews who had believed him, 'If you abide in my word, you are truly my disciples, and you will know the truth, and the truth will set you free.'"

Everyone has an area of life where they engage in "ethical fading." The Bible says, "No temptation has overtaken you that is not common to man" (1 Corinthians 10:13). The sad reality is that we are all guilty of lying from time to time and often do it without realizing it. Where are you most tempted? Know where you are vulnerable and then purpose to stand for the truth.

Take the Challenge

Lying, like stealing, is one of the hardest sins to confess. But, if you want to motivate yourself to tell the truth, make it your personal policy to confess your lies when you are convicted. Take the challenge and purpose that the next time you exaggerate or shade the truth, you will return immediately to the person and confess that you lied. But, before you allow that to happen, consider the possible consequences. Reviewing the repercussions of getting caught can be a healthy way to keep your tongue from speaking lies.

17

Men Memorize the Word

"The mouth of the righteous utters wisdom, and his tongue speaks justice. The law of his God is in his heart; his steps do not slip." (Psalm 37:30–31)

One of the most challenging components of Army boot camp was the monotonous repetition. We were taught how to disassemble the M-16 assault rifle and reassemble it again and again. The drill instructors taught us, and then we taught each other in spontaneous field classes. Every soldier could do the job blindfolded. Then, after firing a couple hundred blank rounds in the field, we cleaned our weapons to brand new condition. The sergeants could detect the slightest speck of carbon. The inspections were brutal. The goal, we were told, was to prepare us for a day when our lives depended on that M-16 not jamming. Then there were the days between range sessions where we drew our weapons from the armory just to clean the already perfectly clean rifles.

I left the Army without ever firing a wartime round. But forty years later, when a friend asked if I could help him figure out how to clean his assault rifle, I recognized the M-16 platform the moment I held it in my hands. I then took his rifle apart in seconds. Even though I never consciously tried to "memorize" how to take apart my weapon, the repetition of basic training helped me remember it for life.

Repetition is one of the most effective ways to memorize information. The Army understood this. Rather than require us to memorize essential tasks, they drilled them through regular repetition.

For Christians, the Word of God is our weapon. It's listed by Paul in Ephesians as our offensive piece of armor—the "sword of the Spirit" (Ephesians 6:17). But before we can effectively deploy the Word, we must first hide it in our hearts. To do that, we can use that military strategy to memorize verses from the Bible—repetition. We need to know the Word like a soldier knows how to field strip his M-16. That requires us to study it again and again and practice using it our entire lives.

There is no excuse for the believer who thinks, *I can't memorize.* If you put the time in, you'll remember. The problem with us is that we don't realize our life depends on memorizing Scripture. The writer of Psalm 119 understood. He wrote, "I have stored up your word in my heart, that I might not sin against you" (v. 11).

Memorize Scripture like a recruit learns to clean his M-16. Don't just try and memorize words, get your hands on the Word and use it. Start with a verse like Proverbs 3:5–6. Repeat it five times in the morning and five times in the evening. Don't worry about trying to memorize it, just read it out loud again and again. Then share it with three to five people you know. Set up a time with a friend to discuss the verses' meaning and ask each other how you can practically apply it in your life. Then meet again two weeks later to ask how you are doing with trusting the Lord with *all* your heart.

John described Jesus as the Word who was with God in heaven but came to earth as a man (John 1:1, 14). So, there is a real sense that as we memorize God's Word we take in the truth of Jesus, the living Word, into our minds. So if you want to know Jesus better, study and memorize the Scriptures. And if you need help, call upon the Spirit of truth that Jesus sent to help "bring to your remembrance all that I have said to you" (John 14:26). So as you work to memorize, pray and ask the Spirit of God to help you.

Then, don't just repeat a verse again and again; ask the Spirit of God to help you live it. Putting it into practice is an important step. The apostle James writes, "Do not merely listen to the word, and so deceive yourselves. Do what it says" (1:22 NIV). No drill instructor worth his salt would think a soldier could learn how to field strip his M-16 from a textbook, without actually doing the hands-on practice. We too must practice the verses we remember if we hope to recall them for a lifelong battle against the evil one.

Get Started

Take time today to meditate on Psalm 119:11: "I have stored up your word in my heart, that I might not sin against you."

Write the above verse on an index card and read it five times in the morning and evening for a week. Look to share it (even if you read it) at least once per day with someone, and set up a time with a Christian friend to discuss the verse and how you can apply it. Once you've got Psalm 119:11 down, add a second verse. You can memorize Proverbs 3:5–6, James 1:21–24, or a verse of your choice.

Take the Challenge

One of the best ways to memorize is to work on a whole chapter of the Bible at once. You can use the same principles we discussed above. Write the chapter down on index cards, one verse per card. Then read a card a day, five times in the morning and five times in the evening. Add a verse every day and look to discuss the new one daily with someone you know. Then, set up a time with a friend to discuss the chapter and ask how you can put it into practice in your life. Choose from Proverbs 3 or James 1 to get started, and you'll remember those chapters.

18

Men Conquer Fear

"The LORD is my light and my salvation; whom shall I fear?
The LORD is the stronghold of my life; of whom shall I
be afraid?" (Psalm 27:1)

The scariest thing you'll ever do in life is face and conquer your fears. Perhaps you've experienced this fundamental test of manliness. Your knees are knocking, your palms sweating, and you realize that if the rope breaks you die. If you fail to pass the test, everyone at work will hear that you didn't pass. If the woman you love says no to your proposal, you'll feel humiliated. Just thinking about life's paralyzing moments is enough to turn the strongest of men into mush.

The mighty King David, who faced the Philistine giant Goliath, didn't fare so well when he later fled from Saul back to Goliath's hometown carrying Goliath's sword. When the servants of King Achish recognized David, he became very much afraid. So, what did David do? He "pretended to be insane in their hands and made marks on the doors of the gate and let his spittle run down his beard" (1 Samuel 21:13). Later David reflected on this moment of his life and realized that God was with him even when he didn't feel the Lord's presence.

> I sought the LORD, and he answered me
>   and delivered me from all my fears.
> Those who look to him are radiant,
>   and their faces shall never be ashamed.

This poor man cried, and the LORD heard him
  and saved him out of all his troubles.
The angel of the LORD encamps
  around those who fear him, and delivers them.

Oh, taste and see that the LORD is good!
  Blessed is the man who takes refuge in him!
Oh, fear the LORD, you his saints,
  for those who fear him have no lack! (Psalm 34:4–9)

The secret to facing our own frailty is trusting an all-powerful sovereign God, rather than ourselves. David conquered his fears by placing his trust in his all-powerful God. It was David who said, "Even though I walk through the valley of the shadow of death, I will fear no evil" (Psalm 23:4).

Jesus said that not a sparrow falls to the ground apart from God's command (Matthew 10:29). The secret to conquering our fears in life is knowing God is in control. He has a plan and is working all things for our good—nothing surprises him (see Romans 8:28; Ephesians 1:11). Consider how God describes himself through the prophet Isaiah.

"Remember the former things, those of long ago; I am God, and there is no other; I am God, and there is none like me. I make known the end from the beginning, from ancient times, what is still to come. I say, 'My purpose will stand, and I will do all that I please.' From the east I summon a bird of prey; from a far-off land, a man to fulfill my purpose. What I have said, that I will bring about; what I have planned, that I will do" (46:9–11 NIV).

Our confidence in life rests on a foundation of trust in our awesome God. So as you face the challenge to provide for your family or disciple your sons or ask for that promotion, remember that God controls your life, your very breath—he alone determines if you will live another day. Greater fears conquer lesser fears. Real men fear God more than they fear life. As a result, they put their trust in God, not themselves. When life gets scary, real men trust God.

Get Started

Take time today to meditate on Isaiah 43:1–2: "But now thus says the LORD, he who created you, O Jacob, he who formed you, O Israel: 'Fear not, for I have redeemed you; I have called you by name, you are mine. When you pass through the waters, I will be with you; and through the rivers, they shall not overwhelm you; when you walk through fire you shall not be burned, and the flame shall not consume you.'"

Make a list of your fears and think through how trusting God can help you conquer your fear. Psalms 23 and 34 are David's prayerful reflections on how he needed to trust God rather than fear. Following David's example, write a prayer to God stating how you will trust him to help you overcome your fears.

Take the Challenge

One of the most common fears people have is sharing their faith with others. Few things accentuate your need to trust God more than sharing the gospel with unbelievers and calling them to trust in God. If you want practice overcoming fear and trusting God, plan a time to go out and share your faith. Who does the Spirit of God want you to share the gospel with? No one comes to mind? No problem, the world is full of unbelievers you can strike up a conversation with. Just go to a local shopping mall, lunch hangout, or other gathering place and pray God would lead you to start a conversation with a total stranger. Need a conversation starter? How about the following: Hi, my name is _____, and I'm asking people about their faith. Do you mind if I ask you a question? What does the Bible say is the only way a person can get to God the Father in heaven? (By the way, the answer can be found in John 14:6). Now go out and conquer your fear by putting your faith and trust in God.

19

Men Take Initiative

"So whoever knows the right thing to do and fails to do it,
for him it is sin." (James 4:17)

In 1940, the German army selected Castle Colditz to hold recaptured Allied officers who had attempted escapes from other prisoner-of-war (POW) camps. Colditz provided a way for officers to wait out the war, free from the dangers of battle. But rather than pass the time hoping for a quick victory and return home, the men of Colditz worked day and night looking for ways to escape and get back into the fight. They were men of initiative.

At the base, the walls of Colditz were seven feet thick. The sheer cliff foundation for the fortress dropped to the river below, which guarded the way of escape. With the nearest Allied force four hundred miles away, recapture or death was the likely outcome if a prisoner made it beyond the walls. POW Patrick Reid described his first glimpse of the fortress as "forbidding enough to make our hearts sink into our boots."[1]

Though it was designated "escape-proof," more than one hundred prisoners found a way to escape beyond the walls, and thirty-two of those men hit "home runs," that is, made it to freedom. Flight Lieutenant Bill Goldfinch and Lieutenant Anthony Rolt win the award for the greatest ingenuity. They drafted plans and then built a full-size glider. The two men planned to pilot the airplane and catapult from atop the castle, launched by the thrust of a bathtub filled with concrete and dropped through holes cut in the castle floors.

The "Cock" measured thirty-two feet from wingtip to wingtip and was assembled behind a false wall. The war ended before the planned launch day and the glider and airship were lost, but not before Lee Carson, a newspaper correspondent, snapped a photo authenticating the audacious story of its clandestine construction.[2] In 2012 Tony Hoskins fabricated a full-size radio-controlled replica. He launched it from atop the castle, in keeping with the original plan. The glider drifted down from Colditz, flew over the Elbe River, and landed safely in a meadow 550 feet below.[3]

Men are created to take initiative. God gave Adam and Eve a broad mission that required Adam to take action. God said, "Be fruitful and multiply and fill the earth and subdue it, and have dominion over the fish of the sea and over the birds of the heavens and over every living thing that moves on the earth" (Genesis 1:28). Ruling and subduing require initiative. The apostle James wrote, "So whoever knows the right thing to do and fails to do it, for him it is sin" (James 4:17). In other words, don't wait to be told what to do! Solomon told his sons, "A slack hand causes poverty, but the hand of the diligent makes rich. He who gathers in summer is a prudent son, but he who sleeps in harvest is a son who brings shame" (Proverbs 10:4–5).

It is the duty of every officer to try and escape if he is captured, and it is the duty of every Christian man to take initiative with regard to the mission of Christ. James tells us to "be doers of the word, and not hearers only" (1:22) and adds that if we take initiative we will be "blessed" (1:25). Jesus said if we want to be like the man who built his house on the rock, we need to take initiative to put his teaching into practice (Matthew 7:24).

Men see a need, take the initiative, make a plan, and spring to action. What about you? Is there a task that you've resisted completing? Is there a repair calling out to be fixed that you've neglected to address? Have you been prompted to return to further your education but haven't taken action? Are there problems at work that no one has asked you to solve, but with a little initiative you could remedy? Problems, repairs, and challenges are all opportunities for the man who takes action. Anytime we address a difficulty or take initiative to solve a problem, we bring glory to God, who created men to take initiative.

Get Started

Take time today to meditate on Proverbs 14:23: "In all toil there is profit, but mere talk tends only to poverty."

Taking initiative is a muscle every man should learn to exercise. The process begins with looking around your world to discover problems that are calling out for solutions. Does the trash overflow every Friday at the office? Take the initiative to solve that problem by taking it out to the dumpster. Think about your week and come up with at least one way you can demonstrate initiative. Make a plan, execute the idea, and solve the problem.

Take the Challenge

Draft a list of all the projects in your work, home, and church that need initiative. You won't see them all, but each man observes the world in which he lives from a different perspective. God will give you eyes to see problems and challenges that you can address. Once you've completed your list, pray over the items, asking God to help you discern which of the issues he is calling you to conquer. Then schedule a time for you to address each challenge in your calendar. Begin your entry with the word *Initiative* to remind you not to dismiss the task when the time arrives to complete it.

20

Men Embrace Team

"Every kingdom divided against itself is laid waste,
and no city or house divided against itself will stand."
(Matthew 12:25)

One day, while hiding from Saul in the cave of Adullam, King David wished for a drink from the well at Bethlehem: "Oh, that someone would give me water to drink from the well of Bethlehem that is by the gate!" (2 Samuel 23:15). He remembered the sweet taste of the water of the well but mourned the presence of the Philistines who controlled the city and held a garrison of troops there. Upon hearing David's longing, three of his mighty men set out to break through the Philistine camp, plunged a bucket down into the well, and brought the water back to David to satisfy his wish. But when David received the water, he poured it on the ground as an offering to the Lord. David explained, "Far be it from me, O LORD, that I should do this. Shall I drink the blood of the men who went at the risk of their lives?" (2 Samuel 23:17).

The loyalty of David's band of mighty men, some of the best warriors in all of Israel, is clear from the story. Yet David refused to partake of the water and be complicit in endangering the lives of his men for his own satisfaction. To honor their sacrifice he poured out the water as an offering to the Lord. David's unselfish move elevated him even more in the eyes of his men because it demonstrated that he was part of the team; though he led the band of mighty men, he should not be singled out above the team.

Good men are team players; they sacrifice their own desires for the good of others. They are willing to give up their own satisfaction for the greater good and unity of the whole. Unity is against our selfish, sinful nature, which is given to complaining and criticism.

When naming what the apostle Paul calls "evident" acts of the sinful nature (Galatians 5:19), half the sins he mentions directly affect unity. Paul lists "enmity, strife, jealousy, fits of anger, rivalries, dissensions, divisions" (v. 20) and warns that "those who do such things will not inherit the kingdom of God" (v. 21).

There is no greater team ever created than the church of Jesus Christ. As members of one body, we're called to offer the same kindness and support to each other that Jesus has extended to us. The Bible compares the members of the church to the stones of a wall, each fit together in perfect harmony by the master stonemason (1 Peter 2:5). Jesus said that the world will know we are his disciples by our love for one another (John 13:35). Division in the ranks destroys that message and threatens God's family.

Later in David's life his son Absalom plotted to steal his father's throne. He spread division through deception. Absalom stood at the gate of the city to intercept those on their way to see the king. He told them, "'your claims are good and right, but there is no man designated by the king to hear you.' Then Absalom would say, 'Oh that I were judge in the land! Then every man with a dispute or cause might come to me, and I would give him justice.' And whenever a man came near to pay homage to him, he would put out his hand and take hold of him and kiss him. Thus Absalom did to all of Israel who came to the king for judgment. So Absalom stole the hearts of the men of Israel" (2 Samuel 15:3–6). But Absalom met with an untimely death as a result of his rebellion.

Many a rebellion begins with a factious word and complaining spirit. Paul calls all those who belong to Christ to "crucify" (kill) any desire that seeks to war against unity (Galatians 5:24). Do you see the seriousness of the sin of divisiveness and look to kill it in your life? How quickly do you give voice to a complaint in your heart against your boss, coworker, pastor, or other leaders? Know that the moment it leaves your tongue, the charge becomes divisive, warring against unity. Blessings come when we stop to think twice before we speak and instead choose to hold our tongues. In Christ, we can be overcomers of a complaining spirit.

Get Started

Take time today to meditate on Ecclesiastes 4:9–10: "Two are better than one, because they have a good reward for their toil. For if they fall, one will lift up his fellow. But woe to him who is alone when he falls and has not another to lift him up!"

Make a list of any complaints you have against your leaders, coworkers, and friends. Then think of any ways you can help join in serving the church as a demonstration of your unity with the body.

Take the Challenge

Often, the very people we complain about could use our loyal help. Consider the list you made above in the Get Started exercise. You can thrust a dagger into the divisiveness of your heart by coming up with ways to serve and help the people you've complained about. If you've spread complaints, go back to those you've complained to and confess your sin. How can you serve and help your boss, pastor, or coworker with whom you are critical? How could you support them among your peers? Make a list of three ways you can foster unity within your spheres of influence. Then serve each person on your list.

21

Men Express Gratitude

"Do all things without grumbling or questioning, that you
may be blameless and innocent, children of God without
blemish in the midst of a crooked and twisted generation."
(Philippians 2:14–15)

The destruction of the Egyptian army at the hand of the Lord
is one of the greatest epic routs of all time. Not a single sword
was raised by Israel. Here is how their post-battle celebration
song described the outcome: "The LORD is a warrior; the LORD is
his name. Pharaoh's chariots and his army he has hurled into the
sea. The best of Pharaoh's officers are drowned in the Red Sea.
The deep waters have covered them; they sank to the depths like
a stone. Your right hand, LORD, was majestic in power. Your right
hand, LORD, shattered the enemy. In the greatness of your maj-
esty you threw down those who opposed you" (Exodus 15:3–7
NIV). But their gratitude didn't last long. In three days they were
grumbling and complaining, first for water then for food.

Complaining is fundamental to our fallen, sinful nature.
Born with the propensity to grumble, we whine about the
weather or anything that doesn't go as planned. We whine when
we don't get enough or when we get too much. We grumble
at life's bad news and can even complain about life's blessings.
Complaining flows from our ungrateful, unbelieving hearts. It
is ultimately a charge leveled against God. When you complain,
you are basically questioning God's wisdom, doubting God's
goodness, and criticizing God's care.

God delivered Israel from the oppression of slavery in Egypt. God brought epic plagues upon Egypt. He led them out of Egypt with a pillar of cloud by day and a pillar of fire by night. Still, when caught up against the Red Sea, rather than ask for help from a God they knew controlled locusts, frogs, gnats, and more, the people grumbled (Exodus 14:11–12). God then opened a way through the Red Sea and swallowed up their Egyptian pursuers after they were safely across. God promised to lead them to a land flowing with milk and honey (3:17). But rather than trust God and ask him for the provisions they needed, the people complained, again and again (Numbers 11). Unfortunately, we're just as quick to complain as they were.

The apostle Paul challenged the Philippians with these words: "Do all things without grumbling or questioning" (Philippians 2:14). His appeal comes after reminding them of the sacrifice of Jesus for our salvation. The gospel is the surest antidote to a complaining spirit. When we remember that the holy Son of God gave up his throne to take on our sin and suffer a horrible death and punishment in our place, our complaints have no place to stand. The gospel is the cure for a complaining spirit. Paul said it like this: "Let your manner of life be worthy of the gospel" (1:27).

And lest you complain against Paul's exhortation, remember that he wrote those words while being imprisoned. It was through his suffering that Paul learned the lesson the Israelites failed to comprehend: "I have learned the secret of facing plenty and hunger, abundance and need. I can do all things through him who strengthens me" (4:12–13).

Rather than rail against God for his imprisonment, Paul entrusted his life to God. The Romans couldn't lay a hand upon him if God didn't allow it. Paul knew God was in control and would strengthen him through the most difficult of circumstances. Paul could see God working through his trial: "I want you to know, brothers, that what has happened to me has really served to advance the gospel" (Philippians 1:12). Still, Paul didn't love suffering and trial; he longed to be with Christ in heaven (v. 23). He looked forward to the day when every tear would be wiped away. But knowing it was God's will for him to remain in the body, he remembered the gospel, put his hope and trust in Christ, and refused to complain. That is what we need to do.

Complaining doesn't secure God's blessing any more than your complaining will get a drill sergeant to reduce your number of push-ups. God has a way of curing our complaining by removing his protective hand and allowing the trials of life to discipline us and lead us back to him. If it were not for the trials he lovingly allows, many of us would turn back to Egypt, just like the Israelites threatened to do. The mature man learns to trust God amid difficulty and thus avoids the loving discipline of the Lord.

Get Started

Take time today to meditate on James 5:8–9: "Establish your hearts, for the coming of the Lord is at hand. Do not grumble against one another, brothers, so that you may not be judged; behold, the Judge is standing at the door."

Make a list of the areas you tend to complain about. Confess the sin of complaining to God and ask him to show you how he is actually working all together for your good (Romans 8:28). Rather than grumble, thank God for the character he is building in your life through the trials and difficulties he has allowed to come your way.

Take the Challenge

Tell your friends you are working on the area of grumbling and complaining. Ask them if they will help point out any complaints or grumblings. Let them know that nothing is off-limits, including work, the weather, and the performance of your sports teams. Choose a favorite charity and purpose to give a ten-dollar donation for each complaint you voice. Don't forget to monitor yourself and the grumbling you offer under your breath that only you (and of course God) can hear.

22

Men Deny Self

"[A]nd he died for all, that those who live might no longer live for themselves but for him who for their sake died and was raised." (2 Corinthians 5:15)

The Crucible is the final test a recruit must endure before becoming a Marine. It's the defining challenge of the Marine basic training designed to test a soldier's endurance, strength, and resolve over fifty-four hours. The exhausting exercise involves forty-eight miles of marching over more than sixty obstacles. Along the way, recruits crawl through mud, repel enemy forces, and challenge each other in boxing matches, all with only six hours of sleep and two prepackaged combat meals. The Crucible is the ultimate denial of comfort and ease for a higher cause—to approve each Marine recruit as battle ready. Every man who seeks to wear the anchor, globe, and eagle emblem of the Marines must deny the pleasures of life and give himself to the Crucible and pass this final test.

Jesus endured his own much greater crucible. It came at the start of his ministry in the wilderness where he fasted for forty days and nights. The test prepared Christ for the battle ahead that he would face at the cross. Where Israel failed to remain faithful to God during their forty-year test in the wilderness, Jesus prevailed and remained steadfast in spite of the wicked temptations thrown at him.

The tempter came to Jesus and challenged him to turn rocks into bread (Matthew 4:3). Though Jesus was weakened from the long fast, his moral resolve did not falter. Jesus replied, "Man shall not live on bread alone, but on every word that comes from the mouth of God" (Matthew 4:4 NIV). The self-denial of fasting weakened his body but strengthened his resolve. When his crucible was over, the trial complete, Jesus rebuked the enemy, and he fled. Later, when faced with the test of the cross, Jesus endured, his final words a testimony of his unflagging faithfulness: "Father, into your hands I commit my spirit!" (Luke 23:46). Jesus died before repeating the last part of the Psalm he quoted, "you have redeemed me, O LORD, faithful God" (Psalm 31:5).

As Christians we are called to the same path of sacrifice that Jesus walked. Jesus said, "If anyone would come after me, let him deny himself and take up his cross and follow me. For whoever would save his life will lose it, but whoever loses his life for my sake will find it" (Matthew 16:24–25).

Every man should learn the benefit of saying no to the demands of his flesh through fasting. The body craves food, and men live to satisfy that most basic craving. But as Jesus declared, "Man shall not live on bread alone." Saying no to hunger is really hard to do, but it helps you put your cravings and desires in submission—the very thing that runs amok when you sin. You can also fast from other life pleasures to put them in their proper place. You can fast from movies, wine, golf, or any other thing that threatens to grow too important and distract you from your call.

The world we live in is broken. We long for Jesus's return, when he will put all things right. When faced with the failings of this world—disease, destruction, and sin—fasting aligns our physical longings with the longings of our heart for the return of the Lord and the restoration of all things. Fasting can also help us focus our prayers for a particular cause, asking God to move on our behalf to bring a bit of restoration into our broken world.

As long as you are healthy, a three-day fast can show a guy just how dependent he is. Fasting helps the strongest of us see the powerful cravings of the flesh and can help train us to say no to the demands of our flesh. Often the desires of our flesh oppose the work of God in our lives (Galatians 5:17). The flesh tells us things like it is okay to put off work until another day, our day is too busy for devotions, or we can put off going to bed to watch another episode. The flesh is always looking for a way to get around life's crucible. Fasting submits the flesh to the command of our will and ultimately under the direction of the Spirit living within every believer.

Fasting is an assumed spiritual discipline in Scripture. Jesus said to his disciples, "and when you fast, do not look gloomy" (Matthew 6:16). He didn't say "if you fast." Fasting is also an offering to God we can make along with prayer. We present our needs to God in prayer, and we demonstrate our dependence upon God alone through fasting. That is why we see fasting and prayer together in Scripture (Luke 2:37; Acts 14:23).

Fasting sounds like a great idea until you decide to begin one. Then you will see just how powerful your flesh can be as you come up with excuse after excuse for why "now" is not a good time to start. But the benefits of saying no to life's most basic cravings can help you during the future tests that you must win over sinful desires. When you fast, take time to focus and dedicate yourself anew to living for God. Winning the mini crucible fasting offers can help ensure that future battles against your flesh will end in victory.

Get Started

Take time today to meditate on Joel 2:12–13: "'Yet even now,' declares the LORD, 'return to me with all your heart, with fasting, with weeping, and with mourning; and rend your hearts and not your garments.' Return to the LORD your God, for he is gracious and merciful, slow to anger, and abounding in steadfast love; and he relents over disaster."

Pick a day when you are off from work and fast from breakfast, lunch, and dinner. Commit the time to prayer. Whenever you're tempted to eat, say no to your desires and freshly pledge your devotion to God. Consider the broken world and what it will be like when Christ returns to make all things new. Take time to reflect and see if there is any area of your life out of balance. Do you have any desires that have grown to occupy too prominent a place? Could you use a little self-denial to rebalance your priorities?

Take the Challenge

Go through your own crucible. Do a three-day fast, followed by a month-long fast from on-screen entertainment. Take the seventy-two hours of your fast to pray and the month away from screen time to read through the four gospels—Matthew, Mark, Luke, and John. Use the time to rededicate your life in service to God.

Men Welcome Adversity

"Behold, I have refined you, but not as silver; I have tried
you in the furnace of affliction." (Isaiah 48:10)

The average NFL football game lasts three hours with com-
mercial breaks, but there is only one hour of game time. Most
of those minutes tick off between plays. In fact, when you add
up the time the ball is in play, the game is only eleven minutes
long.[1] Individual players play far less as they only participate in
half the game—offense or defense—and don't stay on the field
for every play. The quarterback, who is in for most of the offense,
can play less than five minutes and hold the ball for less than
120 seconds in the entire game. In contrast, players train their
bodies and minds for more than sixty hours to prepare for their
important seconds on the field. As my drill sergeant would say
about the hundreds of hours of training in case we had to fight
in a war, "No Pain, No Gain."

The phrase "No Pain, No Gain" is a popularized version
of the wisdom of Benjamin Franklin. He wrote "There are no
gains without pains," in his Poor Richard's almanac in 1745.[2]
But the idea didn't originate with Franklin. God is the author
of this maxim. James, the brother of Jesus, said it this way in his
letter: "Consider it pure joy, my brothers and sisters, whenever
you face trials of many kinds, because you know that the testing of your faith produces perseverance" (James 1:2–3). In other
words, God sends us pains to bring us gains.

There is nothing like a trial to press us into God. When life goes smoothly, it's much easier to forget our constant need for God's grace. He sustains our every heartbeat and our breath. But self-sufficiency is quick to rob us of our dependence upon God. So God, in his wisdom, brings trials to draw us back to him and purify our faith (1 Peter 1:3). The daily trials of life keep us close to God.

When trials come to us, it's essential to remember that God isn't punishing us but disciplining us as sons (Hebrews 12:7). God knows the gains that the pains he brings will produce: "For the moment all discipline seems painful rather than pleasant, but later it yields the peaceful fruit of righteousness to those who have been trained by it" (v. 11). The psalmist understood the good work God did in his life through adversity. He wrote, "Before I was afflicted I went astray, but now I keep your word" (Psalm 119:67).

What do we do when we collapse under the difficulty of our trials? Do we give up? If we fell out of formation in a run, Sergeant Harris would chew off our ear with a few choice words: "Get your sorry butt moving, soldier; you are not dead yet! Don't tell me you can't make it. Get back into formation and keep moving. Move! Move! Move!" It worked every time. Guys found energy and courage they didn't know they had. If you're experiencing a long-standing season of difficulty and have lost courage, the writer of Hebrews has a few choice words for you. Get back into formation and keep running: "lift your drooping hands and strengthen your weak knees" (Hebrews 12:12). Welcome your trials as discipline from a loving Father because "God is treating you as sons" (v. 7).

Men recognize the hand of God behind their trials and learn to welcome adversity. As we just discussed, "For the moment all discipline seems painful rather than pleasant, but later it yields the peaceful fruit of righteousness to those who have been trained by it" (v. 11). In other words, no pain, no gain.

Get Started

Take time to meditate today on 1 Peter 4:12–13: "Beloved, do not be surprised at the fiery trial when it comes upon you to test you, as though something strange were happening to you. But rejoice insofar as you share Christ's sufferings, that you may also rejoice and be glad when his glory is revealed."

Make a list of your trials and the ways they're working for your good. Even the worst of trials force us to call out and depend on God. Remember, we're only going to live in this world eighty years or so, but if we trust the Lord, we'll live in heaven for all eternity. If trials are meant to help us trust in the Lord, then they're accomplishing a great work in our lives. Once you have the list, spend time thanking God for allowing those trials and ask him to work them for good. Then ask God to take them away.

Take the Challenge

Make a list of the ways your trials discourage you and give you cause to give up. Then do the opposite. If you've stopped praying, schedule time to pray. If you've given up on a relationship, press in again with love. If you're immobilized with grief, addiction, sickness, or pain, get up and do the opposite of what your flesh is telling you. Welcome the adversity and fight. Purpose to live in the good of God's grace—you can keep running. Get back into formation and run—don't just tag along the back; push your way to the front and lead. With God's grace, you can do it!

24

Men Never Give Up

"And let us not grow weary of doing good, for in due season
we will reap, if we do not give up." (Galatians 6:9)

Abraham Lincoln was one of the greatest Commanders in
Chief our country has ever known. But, behind Lincoln's
impressive list of accomplishments lies a laundry list of failures. On December 3, 1920, the *Washington Times* republished
a short article entitled "Discouraged?" a front-page review of
the failures of the sixteenth president. The piece ended with this
exhortation: "One failure after another—bad failures—great
setbacks. In the face of all this, he eventually became one of the
country's greatest men, if not the greatest. When you think of a
series of setbacks like this, doesn't it make you feel kind of small
to become discouraged just because you think you are having
a hard time in life?"[1] Lincoln once said, "I find quite as much
material for a lecture in those points wherein I have failed, as
in those wherein I have been moderately successful."[2] Lincoln
understood that failures are often the best preparation for success—for those who don't give up.

Similarly, Winston Churchill's wartime leadership is
credited with saving Europe—not to mention Western civiliza-
tion—from certain defeat by Hitler. I can remember reading a
book on his leadership and being stunned by a chart in the book
which listed Churchill's leadership initiatives. The word *failure*
appears next to seven of them.[3] That chart helped me realize that
even great men fail.

Solomon said, "a righteous man falls seven times, and rises again" (Proverbs 24:16 NASB). Falling isn't the mark of failure; refusing to get up and keep going is. Search through the Bible for men who did not fail, and your search will deliver only one result: Jesus. The Lord knows we are weak and will fail: "he knows our frame; he remembers that we are dust" (Psalm 103:14). Still the Lord calls us to repent, turn away from our sin, and live lives worthy of our repentance. When we fall, the Lord calls us to get up and rejoin the mission. It is only in remaining on the ground that we truly fail.

The apostle Paul wrote, "Do not be deceived: God is not mocked, for whatever one sows, that will he also reap. For the one who sows to his own flesh will from the flesh reap corruption, but the one who sows to the Spirit will from the Spirit reap eternal life. And let us not grow weary of doing good, for in due season we will reap, if we do not give up" (Galatians 6:7–9).

The key, then, is never giving up, but instead rising to rebuild from the ashes of your failures. Rotten fruit is the fertile seedbed for the next season's productive vine. God sprouts significant accomplishments from the bed of our failures. Babe Ruth had to endure more than thirteen hundred strikeouts to be the first to hit seven hundred career home runs.

The humble man accepts his failures as a reflection of his fallibility; the proud man shifts the blame. Pride can also manifest as self-pity for a man who defines himself by his failures. He condemns himself. Though God offers forgiveness to all who repent, and life's opportunities to rebuild abound, the man caught in self-pity rehearses his failures and lives in perpetual unbelief. Unlike the righteous man who rises from his failures to try again, the man trapped in the prison of self-pity refuses to rise up and walk out the open door of opportunity.

What about you? Do you have a sober assessment of your weaknesses and failures? Do you take responsibility when you fall short? Are you willing to walk away from self-pity and give something another try, knowing there is a chance you will fail again? When life gets hard and seems out of control and we feel like giving up, let us remember the words of Paul to the Romans: "And we know that for those who love God all things work together for good, for those who are called according to his purpose" (Romans 8:28). We can stay the course and not give up, knowing that our trials are not beyond God's control or his ability to work for our good.

Get Started

Take time to meditate today on Hebrews 10:36–38: "For you have need of endurance, so that when you have done the will of God you may receive what is promised. For, 'Yet a little while, and the coming one will come and will not delay; but my righteous one shall live by faith, and if he shrinks back, my soul has no pleasure in him.'"

Make a list of your failures and, next to each one, list the ways God can use your failure for his good and one action step you can take to be the righteous man who stands up from his fall to carry on.

Take the Challenge

After creating the list above, look for an opportunity to share it with an accountability partner. Are there areas of life where you need to press in and try again? Are there failures on the list that you've never owned and or taken responsibility for? It's not that we must uncover and confess every past failure, but God will oppose the proud man who seeks to keep significant failures and sins a secret (Proverbs 28:13). It could be the Spirit of God would have you confess and admit to things you are desperately trying to hide.

25

Men Sacrifice

"Truly, I say to you, there is no one who has left house or
wife or brothers or parents or children, for the sake of the
kingdom of God, who will not receive many times more in
this time, and in the age to come eternal life."
(Luke 18:29–30)

On September 6, 1967, Sergeant Rodney Maxwell Davis made
the ultimate sacrifice. He gave up his life to save the lives of
his comrades. His Medal of Honor citation reads, "When an
enemy grenade landed in the trench in the midst of his men,
Sergeant Davis, realizing the gravity of the situation, and in a
final valiant act of complete self-sacrifice, instantly threw himself upon the grenade, absorbing with his own body the full and
terrific force of the explosion."[1] Davis, an African American,
willingly gave up his life to save the lives of five white Marines
he didn't know. Davis demonstrated the finest quality a man
could display with his life—self-sacrifice, even unto death.

The apostle Paul described the sacrifice of Christ in his
letter to the Philippians as the motivation for us to sacrifice for
the sake of others.

> Do nothing from rivalry or conceit, but in humility
> count others more significant than yourselves. Let
> each of you look not only to his own interests, but also
> to the interests of others. Have this mind among your-
> selves, which is yours in Christ Jesus, who, though he

was in the form of God, did not count equality with God a thing to be grasped, but made himself nothing, taking the form of a servant, being born in the likeness of men. And being found in human form, he humbled himself by becoming obedient to the point of death, even death on a cross. (Philippians 2:3–8)

We sacrifice to honor God, knowing that Jesus laid down his life for us as the ultimate sacrifice.

Men give up their seats on a bus to a lady, give up their leisure to work, give up their rest to care for a sick child, give up their money to provide, and give up their lives to defend. For the Christian man, no other quality mirrors Christ more than self-sacrifice.

Jesus promised those who sacrifice for the kingdom of God will receive a reward: "Truly, I say to you, there is no one who has left house or wife or brothers or parents or children, for the sake of the kingdom of God, who will not receive many times more in this time, and in the age to come eternal life" (Luke 18:29–30). Jesus then went on to predict his own suffering and death (vv. 31–32).

Wanting to keep their son's memorial close to home, the Davis family declined to have him interred in Arlington. Rodney was buried in Linwood Cemetery, an African-American graveyard outside the city, because the law didn't allow African Americans to be buried within the city limits of Macon, Georgia.[2] Through the years, Linwood fell into disrepair, Rodney's family moved away, and his grave went untended.

Rodney Maxwell Davis's memorial was overgrown with weeds and nearly forgotten until Randy Leedom, one of the men saved by Davis, visited Linwood to pay his respects. Leedom was appalled by the condition of the memorial and alerted his fellow Marines. Soon the 1st Battalion, 5th Marines veterans' group "sprang into action."[3] Thousands of dollars were raised and the gravesite and cemetery restored. They erected a new memorial to replace the original crumbling cement marker. Today the monument commemorating his sacrifice stands as an example to all men.

Where are you called to sacrifice for the good and benefit of others? Few men will be called upon to give up their lives, but all men are called to model Christ's life, sacrificing self for the good of others.

Get Started

Take time to meditate today on Philippians 3:8–9: "I count everything as loss because of the surpassing worth of knowing Christ Jesus my Lord. For his sake I have suffered the loss of all things and count them as rubbish, in order that I may gain Christ and be found in him, not having a righteousness of my own that comes from the law, but that which comes through faith in Christ."

Make a list of the relationships God has placed you in where you can deny yourself for the good of others and consider their interests above your own. List at least one sacrifice you can make for the good of those relationships. Then purpose to make that sacrifice before the week ends.

Take the Challenge

While anything that we give up for the good of others falls into the category of sacrifice, real sacrifice costs us more than our flesh wants to give. Make a list of three sacrifices you could make that cost you more than your flesh would like you to give. Consider the categories of donating more money, serving more, and giving up more for the good of others.

26

Men Obey God's Commands

"If you love me, you will keep my commandments"
(John 14:15).

The word *listen* is about more than a man's ears; listening involves doing. Whenever Sergeant Harris perceived that our platoon wasn't paying attention, he would shout, "Read my lips!" Harris knew that it was possible to hear a command and never put it into practice.

God sent Samuel to Saul to give him this command: "The LORD sent me to anoint you king over his people Israel; now therefore listen to the words of the LORD. Thus says the LORD of hosts, 'I have noted what Amalek did to Israel in opposing them on the way when they came up out of Egypt. Now go and strike Amalek and devote to destruction all that they have" (1 Samuel 15:1–3). This was Saul's "read my lips" moment. Whenever a prophet tells you to do something accented by "Thus says the Lord," it's best to listen up and get your doing muscles ready.

Unfortunately, Saul did not obey. He gathered an army and attacked Amalek, but he spared the king and only destroyed what was despised and worthless (1 Samuel 15:9). Saul also set up a monument to his accomplishments, which gives you a window into his heart. Bottom line: Saul heard the Word of the Lord, but he didn't obey. He kept the best of the spoils for himself. When Samuel returned, Saul announced, "I have performed the commandment of the LORD" (1 Samuel 15:13), but the bleating of the sheep in the background testified to his disobedience. Saul heard the words of the command, but he did not listen; he did not obey.

The Word of the Lord has come to all men through the Scriptures. It is not enough to read the words or hear them preached on Sunday; we need to listen to what they say, that is, *do* what they say. Only then will your life be true, for as Jesus said, God's "word is truth" (John 17:17). Simply put, men must obey God's Word. Obedience is aligning your life according to the teaching of Scripture. Our obedience to God's commands demonstrates the measure of our love for God (1 John 5:2–4). Jesus said, "If you love me, you will keep my commandments" (John 14:15). But then Jesus went on to say, "And I will ask the Father, and he will give you another Helper, to be with you forever" (John 14:16). We're called by God to obey, but he has given us his Spirit to help us along the way. As we study God's Word, we learn that his commands are not burdensome (1 John 5:3) but lead to abundant life and joy.

Psalm 119 is a symphony acclaiming God's Word. From verse 1 to 176, we learn that God's Word is a light to my path (v. 105), can keep a man blameless (v. 1) and his way pure (v. 9), and give him strength (v. 28) and understanding (v. 99) to make him wiser than his enemies (v. 98). The Word is a comfort in affliction (v. 50), the hope of our redemption (v. 154), and salvation (v. 81). "The sum" of God's Word, the psalmist tells us, is truth (v. 160). The man who aligns his life with the word of truth (2 Timothy 2:15) and does what it says will prosper (1 Kings 2:3; Psalm 1:3).

But a man can know the Word of God, and even quote it well, and still not align his life to God's Word. Those who speak it in public but disregard it in private are hypocrites, like the Pharisees. Jesus condemned them, saying, "Woe to you, scribes and Pharisees, hypocrites! For you are like whitewashed tombs, which outwardly appear beautiful, but within are full of dead people's bones and all uncleanness. So, you also outwardly appear righteous to others, but within you are full of hypocrisy and lawlessness" (Matthew 23:27–28).

The Christian man must align his life to the Word of God. When we hear the Word preached, we need to do more than listen with our ears. When we read a passage in the Bible, we must do more than say "Oh, that's good." We need to obey. Obedience is the active listening Harris commanded when he shouted "read my lips."

Get Started

Take time to meditate today on 1 John 5:3–4: "For this is the love of God, that we keep his commandments. And his commandments are not burdensome. For everyone who has been born of God overcomes the world."

Make a list of three adjustments you can make to better align your life to God's Word. Then pick one area from the three to work on. Write reminders on your calendar over the next three weeks to give you ample reminders.

Take the Challenge

Complete the Get Started exercise above and then share your answer with those Christians who know you the best. Share what you discovered as you answered the questions of the Get Started exercise. Then ask if they see any area of your life or have any wisdom for you that would help you to better understand your weakness or help you overcome it. Ask if they would hold you accountable to accomplish the goals you set.

27

Men Confess Their Failures

"Confess your sins to one another and pray for one another,
that you may be healed. The prayer of a righteous person
has great power as it is working." (James 5:16)

On August 12, 2000, the *Kursk*, a Russian nuclear submarine, suffered a catastrophic accident during a Naval exercise, when an out-of-date practice torpedo exploded. The resulting heat from the fire detonated the remaining live torpedoes, killing all but twenty-three crew members, and drove the sub to the bottom of the Barents Sea. Because the vessel's rescue buoy was intentionally disabled, the sub was not located until the next day. Rather than acknowledge the accident and admit to the leadership failures which caused it, the commanding officers within the Russian Navy and the government denied the catastrophe entirely. Their parade of lies resulted in the loss of the remaining crew members; they survived the explosion and waited in a compartment near an escape hatch for a rescue that never came.

While the Russians ignored the tremor caused by the explosion, experts in the West correctly diagnosed the tragedy. Swedish Admiral Einar Skorgen used a direct phone to call Admiral Andrei Alexandrovich Popov, the commanding officer of the Russian northern fleet, to offer assistance. The Russians declined, saying, "The situation is under control, and we have no need for any assistance."[1] A deadly combination of fear and pride prevented the Russian admiral from confessing the tragic failure and accepting Western aid. Popov lied, for the situation was far from "under control."

The truth was that repeated attempts to reach the survivors had failed. By the time the Russians finally accepted foreign assistance, the NATO divers found the Kursk completely flooded. Once word of the disaster reached the family of the crew, Russia claimed the men died almost instantly—another lie. A note recovered months later from the wreckage, written by Captain Kolesnikov, listed the names of the survivors who waited to be rescued.[2] Kolesnikov's note told the true story that "twenty-three men waited in the ninth compartment, hoping against hope that a new, more humane Russia valued their lives above national pride."[3]

Why is it so difficult to tell the truth regarding our sins, failures, and mistakes? The short answer is pride. Jesus said, "everyone who does wicked things hates the light and does not come to the light, lest his works should be exposed" (John 3:20). Opening up and admitting our faults and taking ownership of failures is one of the most challenging responsibilities for a man to exercise. And yet there is so much grace in the practice of confession. John writes, "If we confess our sins, he is faithful and just to forgive us our sins and to cleanse us from all unrighteousness" (1 John 1:9). Peter wrote, "Clothe yourselves, all of you, with humility toward one another, for 'God opposes the proud but gives grace to the humble.' Humble yourselves, therefore, under the mighty hand of God so that at the proper time he may exalt you" (1 Peter 5:5–6). Humbling ourselves through the practice of confession is the straightest pathway to grace, forgiveness, and change. So why is it that we resist confession?

As sinners, we're wired to blame shift. It began with Adam and Eve after the first sin. When God questioned Adam and asked if he had eaten the forbidden fruit, he blamed his wife (Genesis 3:12). When God then turned to her, she blamed the serpent. What mercy did they squander for adding lies on top of their disobedience? It's important to note that we may be able to lie our way out of a jam with men, but God always knows our guilt. The writer of Hebrews gives us this sobering truth: "no creature is hidden from his sight, but all are naked and exposed to the eyes of him to whom we must give account" (4:13).

Fear of consequences is one of the main reasons we don't confess. Men can build a convincing argument for why they shouldn't confess in light of resulting repercussions. If you commit adultery, it may be logical to say, "I can't confess because the truth will destroy my marriage." But the truth is that the hurt and destruction has already been done. Confession is the first step to restoring the damage.

A sin that remains hidden never goes away. It may hunker down for a while, but it'll usually rise up and find new expression. Confession with repentance is the greatest sin killer and a powerful weapon we can use to defeat sin. God promises to pour out his grace on those who humble themselves (James 4:6). After all, Jesus came into the world to save sinners (1 Timothy 1:15). For the Christian, repentance is not a one-time deal; it is a way of life.

Get Started

Take time to meditate today on Proverbs 28:13: "Whoever conceals his transgressions will not prosper, but he who confesses and forsakes them will obtain mercy." The discipline of confession begins by sharing your weaknesses and confessing the average everyday sins that are easy to hide. You know, you're in a conversation with a coworker, and you knowingly exaggerate a story. Your conscience taps you on the shoulder and tells you that you just lied. What do you do? It's incredibly hard to go back and take full responsibility and say, "I'm sorry, that story I just told you wasn't true. I lied." Think through your past week. If there is a failure you can own by confessing your mistake, lie, or exaggeration, take that step and share it with the appropriate person.

Take the Challenge

It's easy to confess a "little white lie" or exaggeration, but what about that major failure you've been hiding? If you've got one hanging in your closet that you know you should confess, seek pastoral counsel. Disclose your failure and seek advice as to the wisest way to bring it into the light. One of the most significant deterrents to falling into grave sin is holding a strong ethic of confession.

28

Men Hold Their Tongues

"Know this, my beloved brothers: let every person be quick
to hear, slow to speak, slow to anger; for the anger of man
does not produce the righteousness of God."
(James 1:19–20)

US Army General William Mitchell believed air power was
the key to victory in WWI. Mitchell believed a superior air
force was more effective than costly battleships, and he success-
fully administered tests to prove his theories. He commanded
a mass air assault in the Battle of St. Mihiel, where Mitchell
deployed 1,481 Allied airplanes. The attack demonstrated the
capability of a concentrated air assault. Mitchell sent wave
after wave of planes to attack the Germans across battle lines,
destroying their ground power.[1] In time, William Mitchell received dozens of military honors, including the Congressional
Gold Medal, and became regarded as the "father of the United
States Air Force."[2]

But Mitchell could not hold his tongue. Frustrated that the
Army wouldn't adopt his air priorities, he publicly criticized the
military and the White House to *The New York Times* for failing
to establish superior air power. He ignored calls by his con-
temporaries to watch what he said. After the crash of the Navy
helium-filled airship USS *Shenandoah*, Mitchell let his tongue
loose again in public. He said the crash was the "result of
the incompetency, the criminal negligence, and the almost
treasonable negligence of our national defense by the Navy

and the War Departments."[3] President Coolidge personally ordered that charges be filed against Mitchell for insubordination. Mitchell, one of the greatest military strategists, was court-martialed and run out of the military because he could not keep his mouth shut.

Mitchell could've benefited from the wisdom found in the book of James: "Those who consider themselves religious and yet do not keep a tight rein on their tongues deceive themselves, and their religion is worthless" (1:26 NIV). Later, James warns,

> How great a forest is set ablaze by such a small fire! And the tongue is a fire, a world of unrighteousness. The tongue is set among our members, staining the whole body, setting on fire the entire course of life, and set on fire by hell. For every kind of beast and bird, of reptile and sea creature, can be tamed and has been tamed by mankind, but no human being can tame the tongue. It is a restless evil, full of deadly poison. With it we bless our Lord and Father, and with it we curse people who are made in the likeness of God. From the same mouth come blessing and cursing. My brothers, these things ought not to be so. (James 3:5–10)

Lying, gossip, criticism, slander, complaining, and cursing are all sins of the tongue. Perhaps that is why Solomon wrote, "the prudent hold their tongues" (Proverbs 10:19 NIV). What about you? Which of these sins of the tongue do you most struggle with? How often do you complain when things don't go your way? Do you exaggerate the retelling of a story to enhance your reputation? Do you always tell the truth? Does your speech sound different when you're away from Christian accountability? Do you criticize your boss behind his or her back? Do you complain about the length or quality of your pastor's sermons, the song selection for worship, or the latest decision by the elders? Do you feel the freedom to slander public figures who don't follow your political ideology?

Peter quoted King David from Psalm 34:12: "Whoever desires to love life and see good days, let him keep his tongue from evil and his lips from speaking deceit" (1 Peter 3:10). The apostle Paul instructed, "Do not let any unwholesome talk come out of your mouths, but only what is helpful for building others up" (Ephesians 4:29 NIV). And Jesus gave the strictest of warnings. He said, "I tell you that everyone will have to give account on the day of judgment for every empty word they have spoken. For by your words you will be acquitted, and by your words you will be condemned" (Matthew 12:36–37 NIV).

That is precisely what William Mitchell discovered—the hard way.

Get Started

Take time to meditate today on Ephesians 4:29: "Do not let any unwholesome talk come out of your mouths, but only what is helpful for building others up according to their needs, that it may benefit those who listen" (NIV).

There are two things a man can do to help him control his tongue. First, we must think before we speak. Second, we must evaluate our thoughts against God's Word. Before you speak today, put your thoughts through the Ephesians 4:29 speech review.

Take the Challenge

Keep a "watch your tongue" journal. For thirty days, keep a record of every time you violate the principles of godly speech. Record every lie, slander, gossip, and curse. Writing down each "slip of the tongue" will force you to stay aware of your words. Share your weekly progress with an accountability partner and spend time in prayer asking God to help you honor him with your speech.

29

Men Are Easy to Lead

"Obey your leaders and submit to them, for they are
keeping watch over your souls, as those who will have
to give an account. Let them do this with joy and not
with groaning, for that would be of no advantage to you."
(Hebrews 13:17)

Nineteen days after graduating from high school Jerry Curry
volunteered for the Army in response to North Korea's
invasion of South Korea. His father warned him against the discrimination he knew would come, "If you work hard and try
to cooperate, white folks will encourage you to think that you
will get a fair chance to compete and share in the rewards of the
American Dream. Occasionally, that will actually happen."

It wasn't easy for a black man to endure the discrimination
of the Jim Crow years, and it was even harder for a black man
to advance. But Jerry trusted his father's advice, held his tongue,
and did his best to be easy to lead. Jerry did what he was told, as
long as it didn't compromise his Christian values. He followed
the encouragement to attend Army Ranger School and jump
school, and even left his family for six months to finish his bach-
elor's degree. Later, when told an advanced degree was the only
way to be promoted, he traveled two and a half hours, twice a
week, for two years to earn his masters. His willingness to serve
and give himself to each assignment allowed for the expression
of his leadership gifts. Jerry followed the orders and direction of

his superiors all the way to the rank of Major General, and he served on the staff of several presidents.

The writer of Hebrews described good followership this way: "Obey your leaders and submit to them, for they are keeping watch over your souls, as those who will have to give an account. Let them do this with joy and not with groaning, for that would be of no advantage to you" (13:17). Jesus said if you want to become one of the twelve most influential leaders of the greatest teacher of all time you've got to be his follower (disciple) first (Luke 9:23).

It was the Word of the gospel that saved Jerry Curry, and it was his combat New Testament that saved him a second time. During a combat operation in the Vietnam War, a piece of shrapnel from an exploding mortar hit Jerry in the chest, lodging itself in the small New Testament that he carried in his right shirt pocket. Clearly, God had plans for this faithful soldier.

"Do you suppose that you might become a general someday?"[1] Charlene asked her husband Jerry, knowing they both believed God had an important plan for their lives. "If God wills it,"[2] Jerry answered. From the day he enlisted, Jerry Curry entrusted his promotion to the Lord.

While he made sure he was an easy soldier to lead, he did not compromise his convictions, he continued looking for opportunities to share his faith, and he kept his Bible close at hand. At the right time, Jerry was promoted. Though his qualifications were below the mark for promotion to colonel, he was selected because of his outstanding wartime service record.[3]

Get Started

Take time to meditate today on Matthew 23:11: "The greatest among you shall be your servant." Are you easy to lead? Do you find joy in serving those in leadership over you? Make a list of at least three things you can do to make your service a joy to those in leadership over you.

Take the Challenge

Set up an appointment with each of the leaders over you to ask them how you could better serve them and if there is anything you can do to make it easier for them to lead. Then act on those suggestions.

30

Men Encourage

"Therefore encourage one another and build one another up, just as you are doing." (1 Thessalonians 5:11)

On May 13th, 1940, Winston Churchill stood before the House of Commons, newly commissioned by the king. With the invasion of France, the Munich Agreement and Neville Chamberlain's declaration of peace for Europe dissolved like a wisp of smoke broken by the wind. It was at this anxious hour that Churchill bolstered a fearful nation with these encouraging words:

> I would say to the House as I said to those who have joined this government: I have nothing to offer but blood, toil, tears and sweat. We have before us an ordeal of the most grievous kind. We have before us many, many long months of struggle and of suffering.
>
> You ask, what is our policy? I will say: It is to wage war, by sea, land, and air, with all our might and with all the strength that God can give us; to wage war against a monstrous tyranny, never surpassed in the dark and lamentable catalogue of human crime. That is our policy. You ask, what is our aim? I can answer in one word: Victory. Victory at all costs— Victory in spite of all terror—Victory, however long

and hard the road may be, for, without victory there is no survival.

Look again to Churchill's encouragement and you'll not find flattery or platitudes. E*ncouragement* is the skill of building *courage* into the heart of a person—or, in this case, a nation—with skillfully chosen words. Encouragement calls valor to rise from the ashes of anxiety, courage to stand against fear, and faith to form from the rubble of failure. Encouragement tells the truth with inspiration so that, even in the face of great odds, one can embolden a man to rise again to face another day. Men must learn to encourage.

In the close of his letter to the Thessalonians, Paul encourages them, and he calls them to do the same for one another:

> But since we belong to the day, let us be sober, having put on the breastplate of faith and love, and for a helmet the hope of salvation. For God has not destined us for wrath, but to obtain salvation through our Lord Jesus Christ, who died for us so that whether we are awake or asleep we might live with him. Therefore encourage one another and build one another up, just as you are doing. (1 Thessalonians 5:8–11)

Paul's message is that Christian men need encouragement to stand during a trial and in a temptation-filled world as they anticipate the Lord's return. The writer of Hebrews offers a similar charge. He says, "let us consider how to stir up one another to love and good works, not neglecting to meet together, as is the habit of some, but encouraging one another, and all the more as you see the Day drawing near" (10:24–25). Be particularly aware of the other men in your relational circles. Fatherhood and leading in marriage are not easy tasks. Leading as elders in churches is often a thankless job. A timely encouragement for a guy is like filling the gas tank of a car on E. It can keep him on the road for another week. Barnabas spoke up for Paul in Jerusalem (Acts 9:27), encouraging him greatly and living up to his name, which means son of encouragement.

So how well do you encourage those around you? How frequently do you encourage those entrusted to your care and those set above you to lead? When confronting challenges and failure, criticism and charging are the tempting responses, but rarely do they motivate a person toward growth and change. Encouragement infuses faith, and so all men must practice this vital skill.

Christian man, encourage your neighbor, your boss, and your friend. Purpose to encourage anyone you meet that is discouraged by the length of the fight or the enormity of their task.

Get Started

Take time to meditate today on Hebrews 3:13: "Encourage one another daily, as long as it is called 'Today,' so that none of you may be hardened by sin's deceitfulness" (NIV).

Every one of us passes up multiple opportunities to encourage the people around us every day. We live in a world of discouraged people, thirsty for encouragement. Just look around, and you'll see people taking initiative, faithfully completing their tasks and enduring their trials without thanks or a kind word to keep them going. You can make a difference in their lives. Set a goal to encourage three different people. If you get a skilled cashier when you stop for gas or cup of coffee, say something about it. For instance, "I really appreciate how quick you are. You do a great job and demonstrate a strong work ethic." They will probably answer, "Wow, thanks for the encouragement."

Take the Challenge

When it comes to encouragement, most people fall into one of three categories. On the far left you have the complainers, and the indifferent fill out the middle. But the place you want to be is on the right side—an encourager. Strive over the next week to encourage everyone you interact with each day. If you encourage the same person ten times in one day, your words may lose their impact. But if you encourage ten different people once, you will soon gain a reputation as an encourager. Then, as circumstances warrant, encourage folks again and again. A good measure is never to let a day go by where you miss an opportunity to encourage at least one person.

31

Men Disciple

"You then, my child, be strengthened by the grace that is in Christ Jesus, and what you have heard from me in the presence of many witnesses entrust to faithful men, who will be able to teach others also." (2 Timothy 2:1–2)

The greatest battle we face as men is the battle for truth. Our enemy the devil is a deceiver and the father of lies. Jesus said, "He was a murderer from the beginning, and has nothing to do with the truth, because there is no truth in him. When he lies, he speaks out of his own character, for he is a liar and the father of lies" (John 8:44). From his first appearance in the garden and his lies to Eve, Satan has been at work sowing falsehood and undermining God's truth.

Our faith is the most essential manhood skill we pass on and one God directs specifically to men to teach their children (Psalm 78:5; Ephesians 6:4). As men, we live our lives before God and man. The boys growing up around us watch our lives and learn. There is more at stake from the choices that we make than our own life's consequences. Young men tempted by their sinful nature will eagerly adopt our ungodly example or philosophy if we offer one. Godliness requires repetition to stick, but wickedness needs just one demonstration to sanction a young man to give it a try himself.

When you consider that nearly one in four boys grow up without a dad present in their home, you begin to realize the immensity of the problem. "During the 1960-2016 period, the percentage of children living with only their mother nearly tripled from 8 to 23 percent."[1] The call to pass our faith on to the next generation is also a corporate call to the church. Asaph said, "We will not hide them from their children, but tell to the coming generation the glorious deeds of the LORD" (Psalm 78:4). It is time for men to step up to their responsibility to disciple the young men in their homes and to stand in the gap for fatherless homes by passing our faith to the next generation.

Jesus commanded the disciples to pass on what they had learned. "Go therefore and make disciples of all nations, baptizing them in the name of the Father and of the Son and of the Holy Spirit, teaching them to observe all that I have commanded you. And behold, I am with you always, to the end of the age" (Matthew 28:19–20).

The apostle Paul took Timothy under his wing, a young man whose dad was an unbeliever. Paul's exhortations and encouragements toward Timothy provide a great example. He told young Timothy,

> "Let no one despise you for your youth, but set the believers an example in speech, in conduct, in love, in faith, in purity. Until I come, devote yourself to the public reading of Scripture, to exhortation, to teaching. Do not neglect the gift you have, which was given you by prophecy when the council of elders laid their hands on you. Practice these things, immerse yourself in them, so that all may see your progress. Keep a close watch on yourself and on the teaching. Persist in this, for by so doing you will save both yourself and your hearers" (1 Timothy 4:12–16).

In his address to the Corinthians, we see Paul's affection for his young disciple, but we also observe how having trained

Timothy, Paul now deploys him to carry on the work of ministry. "I urge you, then, be imitators of me. That is why I sent you Timothy, my beloved and faithful child in the Lord, to remind you of my ways in Christ, as I teach them everywhere in every church" (1 Corinthians 4:16–17).

While Paul's discipleship of Timothy is that of a pastor raising a younger man into vocational ministry, Paul's efforts still stand as an example for us, for we are all called to pass to the next generation the truth of the gospel and the wonders God has done (Psalm 78:3-4).

Every man should realize that his life stands as a living example before a younger generation. Moses first commanded fathers to uphold the commandments they were called to pass on to their children (Deuteronomy 6:4–6). Our example doesn't just tell them to do something; it shows them how to do it. So we pass on our faith by what we say and by what we do. Men, we are all called to disciple.

Get Started

Take time to meditate today on Matthew 28:18–20: "All authority in heaven and on earth has been given to me. Go therefore and make disciples of all nations, baptizing them in the name of the Father and of the Son and of the Holy Spirit, teaching them to observe all that I have commanded you. And behold, I am with you always, to the end of the age."

Begin by identifying one person in your life you can disciple. If you are a father, then start with your sons and daughters. If you have a younger brother, your mission is also clear. Others should look for younger cousins, nephews, coworkers, or neighbors. Not all discipleship is formal. The most important thing we do is to provide our godly example and invite others to follow. Take time to prayerfully identify the younger men God has placed in your life and purpose to set a good example before them.

Take the Challenge

Take one or two men through *Brave and Bold*, covering one topic per week. As you do, tell stories of your failures and trials and how God, by his grace, has helped you to grow. Discussing one topic per week will provide a six-month discipleship challenge. The brilliance of Jesus's exhortation to go and make disciples is the effect it has on the mentor. As we urge younger men toward manhood, we too are reminded and thus continue to grow. Passing what we've learned to others is a key to staying on course as a godly man ourselves.

A Final Word

Love and Forgiveness: The Greatest Measures of a Man

"So now faith, hope, and love abide, these three; but the greatest of these is love." (1 Corinthians 13:13)

The most significant measure of any man is his capacity to love. In 1 Corinthians 13, Paul tells the believers at Corinth that even if they had all power, faith, and knowledge, but have not love, they are nothing (1 Corinthians 13:2). The same is true of this study. You can read a thousand books, pray for an hour a day, welcome adversity, stay mission-focused, demonstrate responsibility, honor women, and do everything else listed—but without love you won't truly do any of these things.

On the other hand, you can stumble into sin, forget to read or pray, or do any of a hundred things, but demonstrate love toward God and others, and you will be fine. Your love for God will compel you to repent of your sin, and your love for others will compel you toward change. For love calls us toward obedience to God (John 14:15) and kindness toward one another (1 John 4:20-21).

By boot camp graduation time, I had learned the difference between a quality drill sergeant and a power monger. On the surface, they both barked orders and pushed men beyond themselves. The latter found joy in watching the weak fail, but a quality drill sergeant found joy in watching the weak succeed—he had love. Drill instructors do their best to hide their emotions. But if you knew what to look for, you saw it sneak out now and again. Like the time Sergeant Harris ran alongside Simpson to encourage him to keep running. Simpson was the heaviest guy in our platoon. Harris could have pushed him out for failing to keep up. Instead, he encouraged him to keep going and never quit. Harris railed on Simpson, but that helped him keep running. The day Simpson hung with the rest of us for the entire run, Sergeant Harris could not hide his smile. Simpson stood proud along with the rest of us on graduation day. But no man stood prouder than Sergeant Harris.

God, who is the Lord of the universe and the greatest commander of all time, demonstrates for us that authority and love are not mutually exclusive. Love is not a sign of weakness. Love is the ultimate demonstration of greatness. When it comes to choosing a name by which God described himself, God chose love. God proclaimed the name of the Lord to Moses on the mountain with these words: "The LORD, the LORD, a God merciful and gracious, slow to anger, and abounding in steadfast love and faithfulness, keeping steadfast love for thousands, forgiving iniquity and transgression and sin, but who will by no means clear the guilty" (Exodus 34:6–7). The apostle John said it succinctly, "God is love" (1 John 4:16).

So how is it that God can "forgive iniquity" and "by no means clear the guilty"? The answer is found in the greatest expression of God's love of all time, the giving up of his Son to take the penalty for our sins. "For God so loved the world, that he gave his only Son, that whoever believes in him should not perish but have eternal life" (John 3:16). We love others because he first loved us (1 John 4:19).

A Final Word

So the most critical question is, how well do we love? Scripture is clear: love is far more than a fickle emotion that rises out of a warm feeling. Love is a decision to treat fellow sinners with compassion, forgiveness, mercy, and grace, just as God has done for us. And, perhaps most unexpected of all, it is a decision to extend grace even to our enemies (Matthew 5:44).

Jesus said,

> "If you love those who love you, what benefit is that to you? For even sinners love those who love them. And if you do good to those who do good to you, what benefit is that to you? For even sinners do the same. And if you lend to those from whom you expect to receive, what credit is that to you? Even sinners lend to sinners, to get back the same amount. But love your enemies, and do good, and lend, expecting nothing in return, and your reward will be great, and you will be sons of the Most High, for he is kind to the ungrateful and the evil. Be merciful, even as your Father is merciful" (Luke 6:32–36).

The depth of a man's capacity to love can be measured by how freely he forgives. A gospel man holds no grudge nor exacts revenge, for he is aware of the immeasurable sin debt he has been forgiven. Jesus made this connection in rebuking the Pharisees. He said, "he who is forgiven little, loves little" (Luke 7:47). Paul ties the command to forgive back to the cross. "Be kind to one another, tenderhearted, forgiving one another, as God in Christ forgave you. Therefore be imitators of God, as beloved children. And walk in love, as Christ loved us and gave himself up for us, a fragrant offering and sacrifice to God" (Ephesians 4:32–5:2).

So demonstrating God's abounding love is forgiving the friend who forgot to follow through on his promise for the third time. Or forgiving a coworker who lied and gossiped about you. Or forgiving a neighbor who borrowed a tool but didn't return it. Or any of a thousand other offenses committed against you. Love doesn't pretend those things didn't happen. Instead, love calls us to forgive by embracing the hurt and or loss caused by the transgression. Love covers over an offense so that we never need to bring it up again. Love allows us to not treat a person as their sin deserves, but instead put their sin as far as the east is from the west. That is how God has loved us, so abounding love is a trait all men should aspire to display throughout their lives. And this is only possible if you know the depth of Jesus's love toward you. He must sustain your love with his steadfastness.

Perhaps you've completed the thirty-one challenges listed before this last and greatest challenge to love. Or you may have skipped to this final section to see how this book ends. In any case, take the challenge to go back through the list of the thirty-one qualities of a man and be sure that as you look to conquer each one, that you always put on love, which is the greatest of all (1 Corinthians 13:13). Paul gave the fledgling Colossian church a list of qualities he wanted them to follow. He listed holiness, humility, patience, forgiveness, and more, and then capped it off with these words, which are a fitting way to complete this study:

> And above all these put on love, which binds everything together in perfect harmony. And let the peace of Christ rule in your hearts, to which indeed you were called in one body. And be thankful. Let the word of Christ dwell in you richly, teaching and admonishing one another in all wisdom, singing psalms and hymns and spiritual songs, with thankfulness in your hearts to God. And whatever you do, in word or deed, do everything in the name of the Lord

Jesus, giving thanks to God the Father through him.
(Colossians 3:14–17)

The church needs men. While we should beware of simply affirming every cultural expression of manhood as biblical, we should nevertheless seek to champion men. Jesus proved the world could be changed by a handful of common unlearned fishermen (Acts 4:13). These simple men, and the converts who joined them, by the power of the Spirit of God who filled them, turned the world upside down (Acts 17:6). God is yet at work today, looking for a few good men (2 Chronicles 16:9) who are ready to carry on his mission and be used of him to change the world. Dear man, take up the charge and be counted as one of them.

Acknowledgments

A book like this would not be possible without the help of my friends and family. I want to thank my wife and children for listening to me read through my drafts for this book, again and again. I'm grateful for the time Andrew Kalvelage and Leo Parris took to read through my first draft and offer essential edits. A special shout-out to the drill instructors and officers of the United States Army who transformed this 140-pound weakling into an officer. Much appreciation goes to the New Growth Press team who worked to help me shape this resource.

Finally, I would like to thank the three pastors God used most to disciple me in my formative years: Dave Harvey—I still remember the day you gave me the book *The Measure of a Man* to read, which started my spiritual discipleship. Bill Patton—I am grateful for the way God used your preaching to pour my spiritual foundation. And Alan Redrup—thank you for modeling love toward God's people and demonstrating selfless pastoral care. God used your example to help soften the edges of this Army guy and prepare me for ministry.

Endnotes

Introduction

1. Jacob Sobolev, "How Much Money Does The Average Person Spend On Video Games?," *Gaming Shift*, https://gamingshift.com/how-much-money-does-the-average-person-spend-on-video-games/.

Chapter 1

1. Including this illustration is not meant to be an affirmation of Lincoln's saving faith. Historians debate the particulars of Lincoln's faith, but it seems clear to me that Lincoln was a God-fearing man in the least, with a measure of understanding that God is sovereign, Lord of all, and yet willing to hear our prayers.

2. John D. Wright, *The Oxford Dictionary of Civil War Quotations* (New York: Oxford University Press, 2006), 280.

3. A. W. Tozer, *The Knowledge of the Holy* (New York: Harper Collins, 1978), 1.

Chapter 3

1. Army.Mil Features, "Doss, Desmond T.," https://www.army.mil/medalofhonor/keeble/medal/citations20.htm.

2. Transcribed from Desmond's interview posted before the credits of the movie *Hacksaw Ridge* (2016).

Chapter 4

1. Nick Foles, Joshua Cooley, *Believe It: My Journey of Success, Failure, and Overcoming the Odds* (Carol Stream, IL: Tyndale, 2018), 124.

2. Foles, 124.

3. Foles, 215–16.

Chapter 8

1. Alvin York, *Sergeant York and the Great War* (Bulverde, TX: Mantle Ministries, published in conjunction with Vision Forum, repub. 1998), 169.

Chapter 9

1. Marguerite Ward, CNBC Make It, "Warren Buffet's reading routine could make you smarter, science suggests," November 16, 2016, https://www.cnbc.com/2016/11/16/warren-buffetts-reading-routine-could-make-you-smarter-suggests-science.html; Steve Jordan, Omaha World-Herald, "Investors earn handsome paychecks by handling Buffet's business," April 28, 2013, https://www.omaha.com/money/investors-earn-handsome-paychecks-by-handling-buffett-s-business/article_bb1fc40f-e6f9-549d-be2f-be1ef4c0da03.html.

2. Search "Recommended Reading" at https://www.christianitytoday.com; https://www.thegospelcoalition.org; see also "Book Reviews" at https://www.challies.com.

Chapter 10

1. Sean McLachlan, *Underground Warfare in World War I*, "The Mines of Messines" (Ann Arbor, MI: Charles River Editors, 2017).

2. McLachlan.

Chapter 11

1. Sun Tzu, *The Art of War*, trans. Ralph D. Sawyer (CreateSpace, Black and White Classics, 2014), 8.

2. Brian Hedges, TGC, "Our Most Neglected Spiritual Discipline," August 6, 2018, https://www.thegospelcoalition.org/article/spiritual-discipline-watchfulness/.

Chapter 16

1. NBC News, "Air Force Fires Nine Commanders in Nuclear Cheating Scandal," March 27, 2014, https://www.nbcnews.com/news/us-news/air-force-fires-nine-commanders-nuclear-cheating-scandal-n64106.

2. Stephen J. Gerras and Leonard Wong, *Lying to Ourselves: Dishonesty in the Army Profession* (Carlisle, PA: U.S. Army War College Press, 2015), 2.

Chapter 19

1. P. R. Reid, *Colditz: The Full Story* (London: Macmillan Limited, 1984), 24.

2. Reid, 24, caption above the photo of the Colditz glider.

3. Tony Hoskins, *Flight from Colditz* (Barnsley, S. Yorkshire: Frontline Books, 2016), 150.

Chapter 23

1. David Biderman, "11 Minutes of Action," *Wall Street Journal*, updated January 15, 2010.

2. The Franklin Institute, "Benjamin Franklin's Famous Quotes," https://www.fi.edu/benjamin-franklin/famous-quotes.

Chapter 24

1. Library of Congress, *Washington Times*, December 3, 1920, image 24, https://chroniclingamerica.loc.gov/lccn/sn84026749/1920-12-03/ed-1/seq-24/.

2. Scott Sandage, *Slate*, "I Have Never Been Up," May 28, 2014, https://slate.com/business/2014/05/abraham-lincoln-failure-at-50-why-the-myth-is-so-persistent-and-powerful.html.

3. Steven Hayward, *Churchill on Leadership* (Rocklin, CA: Prima Lifestyles, 1997), 24.

Chapter 25

1. Congressional Medal of Honor Society, "Stories of Sacrifice: Rodney Davis," http://www.cmohs.org/recipient-detail/3255/davis-rodney-maxwell.php.

2. Maria Smith, Explore Georgia, "Four African American Military Memorials You Have to See," September 2018, https://www.exploregeorgia.org/things-to-do/article/4-african-american-military-memorials-you-have-to-see.

3. Phil Gast, CNN, "Always faithful: Marine veterans tend to hero's grave, cemetery," November 12, 2012, https://www.cnn.com/2012/11/09/us/vietnam-veteran-cemetery/index.html.

Chapter 27

1. Robert Moore, *A Time to Die: The Untold Story of the Kursk Tragedy* (New York: Crown, 2003), 104.

2. Ramsey Flynn, *Cry from the Deep: The Sinking of the Kursk, the Submarine Disaster That Riveted the World and Put the New Russia to the Ultimate Test* (New York: HarperCollins, 2004). See photographic insert of Kolesnikov's note.

3. Flynn, 186.